D1049500

DARLENE ZSCHECH

EXTRAVAGANT WORSHIP

BETHANYHOUSE
Minneapolis, Minnesota

Published by Bethany House Publishers
11400 Hampshire Avenue South
Bloomington, Minnesota 55438
www.bethanyhouse.com

Bethany House Publishers is a division of
Baker Publishing Group, Grand Rapids, Michigan.

Printed in the United States of America

ISBN 0-7642-0052-6 (Paperback)
ISBN 0-7642-2751-3 (Hardcover)

Library of Congress Cataloging-in-Publication Data

Zschech, Darlene.
    Extravagant worship : holy, holy, holy is the Lord God Almighty who was and is, and is to come / by Darlene Zschech. — Rev. ed.
        p. cm.
Includes bibliographical references.
        ISBN 0-7642-0052-6 (pbk.) — ISBN 0-7642-2751-3 (hardback : alk. paper)
        1. Public worship. I. Title.
BV15.3 .Z74   2002
264—dc21   2002009658

HOLY, HOLY, HOLY

IS THE LORD

GOD ALMIGHTY,

WHO WAS, AND IS,

AND IS TO COME. . . .

REVELATION 4:8

ACKNOWLEDGMENTS

There are a number of amazing people whose names need to appear in flashing lights on this page . . . as this book would not have happened without them.

JOSH BONETT

Your incredible support and belief in Mark and me has enabled us to actually achieve some of the things that we continually dream of. Thank you for your tireless effort and thank you for taking this book from my heart and beautifully putting it into print! We love you.

MIFFY SWAN

What an awesome woman you are! You make this journey so wonderful for Mark and me. Thank you for literally "running the race" with us. We love you.

MELINDA HOPE

Thank you, my darling friend, for releasing me. There is not a day that goes by that I don't thank God for our "miracle" day. Mark and I, and the girls, love and value you more than you know.

JULIAN SYLVESTER

Thanks, buddy. Whatever it takes, that is your life banner, go for it!

CRIS BOLLEY

Thank you, beautiful lady, for believing in this project enough to allow this fledgling writer to realize her potential . . . you are a pure gift.

Thank you to all the people who helped us put this together: Simone Ridley, Tam Tickner, Steve McPherson, Erica Crocker, Mark Hopkins, Susan Sohn, Robert Fergusson, and Emerald Press. What a team!

THANK YOU

TO MY PRECIOUS LORD

I pray that my life is expressed as a thank-you to you, for words don't
do justice to my depth of love and adoration. I am and
forever will be yours.

TO MY DARLING MAN, MARK

Your strength and your dedication to Christ are what attracted me to
you in the first place. (Oh, and the good looks didn't hurt either!) Thank
you for releasing me and believing in me. Thank you for giving me
wings to fly. But mostly, thank you for loving me like you do.
I love you.

TO MY GIRLS

My heart's treasure, Amy, Chloe, and Zoe Jewel. You are all beautiful
beyond description, inside and out. I count it a privilege to be your
mum. I adore you. Thank you for your patience while I wrote
and wrote and wrote. . . . Love, Mummy

Thank you to our awesome church family, Hillsong Church, the greatest church on the planet! And to our pastors and friends, Brian & Bobbie Houston, Stephen & Donna Crouch, George & Margaret Aghajanian, and the list goes on and on. Your commitment to Christ is inspiring, and our commitment to each other is something I value more than I can say. With all my love . . .

TO THE WORSHIP AND CREATIVE ARTS TEAM

To serve the King alongside such fine men and women of God is one of my favorite things in life. You have taught me so much. I honor and love you all. Remember, all of our greatest days are still ahead.

Love you,

Darlene

ENDORSEMENTS

DON MOEN

God is using Darlene to impact the way people worship all around the world. My family and I have been impacted by her ministry and her passion for the presence of God. More than a gifted songwriter and singer, Darlene is a true leader who is passionate about worshiping the Father in spirit and in truth and is committed to raising up others all around the world to do the same. She is real, transparent, and vulnerable as a worship leader, but more important, she is the same person when she is not in front of thousands. I am honored to endorse Darlene's ministry. As you read this book, I know you will never be the same again.

DR. R.T. KENDALL
WESTMINSTER CHAPEL

When I first began singing Darlene's songs, I knew there was a very unusual anointing on her, but I was not prepared for how impressed I would be when I personally witnessed her leading worship.

MICHAEL YOUSSEF
LEADING THE WAY WITH DR. MICHAEL YOUSSEF

God has blessed Darlene with great gifts and a godly spirit. Darlene's faith has allowed her to minister to countless people. God's hand is surely on this woman's ministry.

MICHAEL W. SMITH
SINGER AND SONGWRITER

Darlene's passion for the Lord and for worshiping Him is clearly heard through her music and song. Be inspired as you read treasures from the heart of a true worshiper.

FOREWORD

BRIAN HOUSTON

Senior Pastor, Hillsong Church

I remember the day Darlene Zschech led worship in our church for the very first time. It actually wasn't all that long ago. After many years of faithfully serving in the choir and singing with our worship team, she took that one bold step forward and has subsequently emerged as one of the most influential praise and worship leaders in the world today.

Her life and ministry are an inspiration to millions, and her most renowned song, "Shout to the Lord," continues to be one of the most popular worship songs today. The very first time I heard it, I knew it was destined to be a great song, but who would have thought it would be sung before the president of the United States, in the Vatican, and by thousands of congregations all over the world!

I love what God has done in Darlene's life so far and I know He has so much more in store for her. Yet what truly blesses me is that she is the same person whether she is on or off the platform. She remains the same gracious, humble woman whose heart has always been to worship and glorify God.

As senior pastors of Hillsong Church, my wife, Bobbie, and I are blessed to be in partnership with Mark and Darlene. Not only do we share a close, intimate friendship with them as a family but we also recognize that they are awesome leaders in the kingdom, committed to touching heaven and changing earth.

If you long to become an extravagant worshiper, then this book will inspire you, as Darlene shares her journey to attain her foremost desire and passion: to be an extravagant worshiper herself!

God bless,

Brian Houston

CONTENTS

INTRODUCTION

At the tender age of fifteen, I committed my life to the Savior of the world, Jesus Christ. Since that moment, His plan for me has continued to unfold as I continue to learn daily that Jesus is both my Lord and my best friend. Along my journey of discovery, I have had many internal struggles to overcome, many lessons to learn, and countless religious ideas to "unlearn." But more important, I have also come to understand and value the power of becoming someone who is committed to praising God at all times, whose passion to worship the King is unquenchable, and whose single desire is found in Psalm 73:25–26:

Whom have I in heaven but you?
And earth has nothing I desire besides you.
My flesh and my heart may fail,
but God is the strength of my heart
and my portion forever.

Since 1986 God has allowed me the honor and privilege of being part of the praise team at Hillsong Church outside of Sydney, Australia. I have also had the privilege of leading the Worship and Creative Arts Department since 1996. What an incredible journey it has proven to be! It has definitely been a time in my life that was "way beyond anything I could ask or think." When our songs, such as "Shout to the Lord," began to spread through worship services throughout the world, our sphere of influence at Hillsong also increased to global proportions. Countless people have since asked me to put pen to paper and explain some of the things that truly matter in our praise and worship department here in Australia.

It is my intention to detail in this book some of the principles that we, as a worship team, cling to and refuse to relinquish. I certainly don't have all the answers, as my own journey is still unfolding before me. But as I share the vision that has been given to me for praise and worship, I trust you will hear my heart as one who is not satisfied by making magnificent music or singing beautiful songs, but that you will see my passion to advance the kingdom all the days of my life.

My heart's desire is that as God searches the earth, He will find me to be an extravagant worshiper. And now that this book has found its way to you, I pray it will establish this quest to be an extravagant worshiper in your heart too.

With all my love,

Darlene Zschech

PART ONE

THE EXTRAVAGANT *Worshiper*

Chapter One

EXTRAVAGANT WORSHIP

EXTRAVAGANT
WORSHIP

Everyone in town knew her as a sinful woman, but her selfless display of extravagant worship changed how everyone remembers her now. Jesus was in Bethany, reclining at the table in the home of a man known as Simon the Leper. "When [she] learned that Jesus was eating at the Pharisee's house, she brought an alabaster jar of perfume, and as she stood behind him at his feet weeping, she began to wet his feet with her tears. Then she wiped them with her hair, kissed them and poured perfume on them" (Luke 7:37–38).

Imagine the depth of this woman's tears being enough to clean the dusty feet of Jesus! Imagine the gratitude that moved her to boldly display her devotion and adoration of the Man reclining at the table. She had heard Him teach of the kingdom of heaven. She had understood the heart of the Lord. She had seen the miracles He had done. She had been delivered from her old way of life through His loving acceptance of her.

With tears flowing from a sobbing heart, she washed the Lord's tired feet and wiped away the soil with the tresses of her hair. Then she perfumed His feet with oil from her alabaster jar that was valued at a year's wages. Her

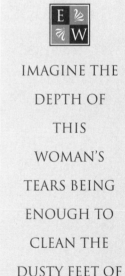

IMAGINE THE
DEPTH OF
THIS
WOMAN'S
TEARS BEING
ENOUGH TO
CLEAN THE
DUSTY FEET OF
JESUS!

love for Jesus knew no bounds. When the others voiced their disapproval of her extravagance, Jesus said, "Leave her alone. She has done a beautiful thing to me."

Oh, for the opportunity to kiss the beautiful feet of Jesus. . . .

As the year 2000 approached, I felt the Holy Spirit had given me the phrase "Extravagant Worshipers" to use as a banner over our department. As part of our weekly rehearsals at Hillsong, we attend teaching nights, and everything that was taught during that year was on this central theme. Our hunger for more of God had fueled the year in a magnificent way, and by the end of that first year I was excited at what 2001 would bring.

THE CAUSE OF CHRIST PUMPING AWAY IN OUR VEINS SHOULD CAUSE EXTRA-ORDINARY PRAISE TO THE FATHER.

Then one quiet moment in prayer, the Lord gently whispered in my ear, *Daughter, you're not an extravagant worshiper yet.* When one hears God say something like that, one humbly listens! So I realize I am not there yet; our team is not there yet; and if we are to continue to call ourselves "extravagant worshipers," I understand that we have a long way to go.

So what does it mean to be an extravagant worshiper?

Webster's Collegiate Dictionary defines the word *extravagant* as "**2 a:** *exceeding the limits of reason* **b:** *lacking in moderation, balance, and restraint (praise)* **c:** *extremely or excessively elaborate* **3 a:** *spending much more than necessary* **b:** *profuse, lavish.*" The Holy Spirit is calling us to excessive worship. We're to be overgenerous in our praises to God. Extravagant worship means to be elaborate in our offering of admiration to Him; our worship is to be over and above reasonable limits previously established.

The cause of Christ pumping away in our veins should cause extraordinary praise to the Father. I long to worship Jesus as did the woman with the alabaster jar of perfume! Excessive, abundant, expensive, superfluous, lavish, costly, precious, rich, priceless, valuable . . .

Jesus knew the woman who anointed Him with her precious perfume fully understood that she had been forgiven for terrible sins. Jesus explained this love she had for Him to Simon the Leper, telling him a parable about two servants who were forgiven for debts by their Master. One owed him a little; the other owed him much. Jesus continued the story:

> *"Neither of them had the money to pay him back, so he canceled the debts of both. Now which of them will love him more?"*
> *Simon replied, "I suppose the one who had the bigger debt canceled."*
> *"You have judged correctly," Jesus said.*
> *Then he turned toward the woman and said to Simon, "Do you see this woman? I came into your house. You did not give me any water for my feet, but she wet my feet with her tears and wiped them with her hair. You did not give me a kiss, but this woman, from the time I entered, has not stopped kissing my feet. You did not put oil on my head, but she has poured perfume on my feet. Therefore, I tell you, her many sins have been forgiven—for she loved much. But he who has been forgiven little loves little."*
> *Then Jesus said to her, "Your sins are forgiven."*
> *The other guests began to say among themselves, "Who is this who even forgives sins?"*
> *Jesus said to the woman, "Your faith has saved you; go in peace"*
> *(Luke 7:42–50).*

When we stand before the Lord to worship Him, we are to worship Him in truth. To do so, we must ask ourselves, "How big are the debts

Jesus canceled for me? How generous was He toward me when considering the pain my sins inflicted upon Him? How much thanks do I owe Him for canceling the consequences of my past? Am I overgenerous with my worship? Do I exceed reasonable limits when praising Him? Or am I merely doing what is required, merely fulfilling the basic level of commitment? Am I simply trying to earn my right of passage?" If our worship is spiritual and truthful, we will search our souls and appraise the value we place on His love for us. What can we bring to the altar that represents extravagance?

I have had the honor of meeting some extravagant worshipers during my lifetime:

Among them is a young couple in our church who lost their young daughter through sickness, yet they worshiped their King through overwhelming grief and are still doing so today.

A young man who was left paralyzed from his waist down through an accident was quickly back in our church services. With tears running down his face, his arms stretched heavenward, and his heart loving Jesus, he worshiped His Savior with extravagant thanksgiving.

A friend of mine, a young married mother of four little ones, whose husband is in our worship team, is always in church, always early, always full of joy, and always found full of extravagant praise for her Lord.

The *Oxford English Dictionary* describes *extravagant* as "wasteful." This word particularly grabbed my attention, for one of the most beautiful accounts of extravagant worship in the Bible is this story of how the gift of perfume from the sinful woman was considered "wasteful" by those around her. But as she poured out her costly perfume from the alabaster jar, she must have wished she had even more to give Him. As she poured out her tears in offering, He washed away her brokenness. As she loved extravagantly, He forgave extravagantly. Her action of elaborate love toward her Lord is a powerful example of true, heartfelt worship. Her act of worship had nothing to do with music or song, but it had all to do with being extravagant in devotion to her Savior.

What is worship, and what are we doing when we worship? True worship, the kind of worship that God seeks, is described in John 4:23–24: "Yet a time is coming and has now come when the true worshipers will worship the Father in spirit and truth, for they are the kind of worshipers the Father seeks. God is spirit, and his worshipers must worship in spirit and in truth."

I have meditated on that Scripture for many hours. I understand true worship to be when one's spirit adores and connects with the Spirit of God, when the very core of one's being is found *loving* Him, lost *in Him.* True worship is not about the songs being sung; it is not about the size of the band; it is not about the size of the choir. Although music is a wonderful expression of worship, it is not in itself the *essence* of it. The core of worship is when one's heart and soul, and all that is within, adores and connects with the Spirit of God. In fact, regardless of how magnificent the musical moments are, unless one's heart is fully engaged in the worship being expressed, it is still only music. The

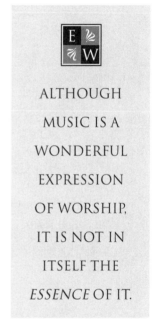

ALTHOUGH MUSIC IS A WONDERFUL EXPRESSION OF WORSHIP, IT IS NOT IN ITSELF THE *ESSENCE* OF IT.

song of a pure heart that is yearning for more of God and less of one-self is the music that holds the key to many victories and delights the heart of our King.

I would love to have met Mother Teresa. She was an extravagant worshiper. One of her favorite hymns, "O Jesus, Jesus, Dearest Lord," reflects the heartbeat of this godly woman. The actions of her life supported the sincerity of her worshipful heart when she sang these words:

O JESUS, JESUS, DEAREST LORD!

FORGIVE ME IF I SAY,
FOR VERY LOVE, THY SACRED NAME
A THOUSAND TIMES A DAY.

I LOVE THEE SO I KNOW NOT HOW
MY TRANSPORTS TO CONTROL;
THY LOVE IS LIKE A BURNING FIRE,
WITHIN MY VERY SOUL.

O WONDERFUL THAT THOU SHOULDST LET
SO VILE A HEART AS MINE
LOVE THEE WITH SUCH A LOVE AS THIS
AND MADE SO FREE WITH THINE.

FOR THOU TO ME ART ALL IN ALL,
MY HONOR AND MY WEALTH,
MY HEART'S DESIRE, MY BODY'S STRENGTH,
MY SOUL'S ETERNAL HEALTH.

WHAT LIMIT IS THERE TO THIS LOVE?
THY FLIGHT, WHERE WILT THOU STAY?
ON, ON! OUR LORD IS SWEETER FAR
TODAY THAN YESTERDAY.

—FREDERICK W. FABER (1814–1863)

CREATED TO WORSHIP

Isaiah 43:7 says that God created us for His glory. " 'You are my witnesses,' declares the Lord, 'and my servant whom I have chosen, so that

you may know and believe me and understand that I am he. Before me no god was formed, nor will there be one after me. I, even I, am the Lord, and apart from me there is no savior' " (Isaiah 43:10–11). First Chronicles 16:28–29 says, "Ascribe to the Lord, O families of nations, ascribe to the Lord glory and strength, ascribe to the Lord the glory due his name. Bring an offering and come before him; worship the Lord in the splendor of his holiness."

EVEN IF YOU ARE PART OF A WORSHIP TEAM, YOUR MOST GLORIOUS MOMENTS OF WORSHIP SHOULD BE OFF THE PLATFORM WHEN YOU ARE ALONE WITH GOD.

Our worship pleases the Lord. There is real strength when believers bring a corporate offering of praise to God in the church. I love the sense of storming heaven with our praise when we unify in faith. I love when we, the body of Christ, can just *be* together in His magnificent presence. God's Word encourages believers to continue meeting together, saying, "And let us consider and give attentive, continuous care to watching over one another, studying how we may stir up (stimulate and incite) to love and helpful deeds and noble activities. Not forsaking or neglecting to assemble together [as believers], as is the habit of some people, but admonishing (warning, urging, and encouraging) one another, and all the more as you see the day approaching" (Hebrews 10:24–25 AMP).

But also we must each worship our King in that secret place, that intimate time, one-on-one, as a lover of Christ. There should be times of worship that only you and the Lord will ever know about. Even if you are part of a worship team, your most glorious moments of worship should be off the platform when you are alone with God. Heartfelt intimacy is private, and your most precious time with your best friend is not in the public moments. Moments alone with God should be revered.

When Jesus came to the village where Martha lived, she opened her home to Him. Her sister Mary (the same one who later anointed Jesus with perfume) sat at the Lord's feet, listening to what he said. But Martha was distracted by all the preparations that had to be made. Eventually she came to Jesus and asked, " 'Lord, don't you care that my sister has left me to do the work by myself? Tell her to help me!' 'Martha, Martha,' the Lord answered, 'you are worried and upset about many things, but only one thing is needed. Mary has chosen what is better, and it will not be taken away from her' " (Luke 10:40–42).

We can understand Martha's concern. She was asking, "Lord, don't you care? Don't you love me for all that I am doing for you?" Of course God cares—and He cares that we learn the only service to Him that is needed. Mary chose to be in the presence of God; she chose to sit at His feet, to spend time in the Word of God. Mary chose what is most necessary.

There is no substitute for time spent alone with God; no substitute for a relationship with Christ. Singing lovely songs *about the Lord* is fantastic, but it is not enough. To worship is to speak *to the Lord* with words full of adoration. To worship God is to bow down to Him, to revere Him, and to hold in awe His beauty. I see worship as a kiss toward heaven.

Worship is a verb, defined as "regard with great or extravagant respect, honor, or devotion." It is an active expression of our love toward God. It is vibrant and visible by our deeds and not only by the words we speak. Worship involves the giving of ourselves totally to the Lord. Worship is neither a ritualistic activity nor a musical emotion. It embodies and reflects the selfless generosity of Christ. Worship is a movement of our hearts, our thoughts, and our wills toward God's heart, thoughts, and will.

But ye are a chosen generation, a royal priesthood, an holy nation, a peculiar people; that ye should show forth the praises of him who hath called you out of darkness into his marvellous light.
(*1 Peter 2:9* KJV)

WORSHIP IS A VERB, DEFINED AS "REGARD WITH GREAT OR EXTRAVAGANT RESPECT, HONOR, OR DEVOTION."

Worship Is a Lifestyle

Worshiping our Savior, Jesus Christ, is fundamental to living a faith-filled, Spirit-led, Christian life. There are countless, conflicting opinions as to how we actually worship the Lord. There are multiple worship methods, plans, and styles that vary among cultures and geographic boundaries. The Lord enjoys the diversity of sincere worship when expressed through His Spirit and in truth. Worship should be a way of life, with many facets of expression.

The insistence that there is only one way to worship God has often left the body of Christ confused, fragmented, and frustrated. Some worship leaders declare that a certain defining style of worship is the only correct way to worship the Lord, but that is a narrow view of His inexhaustible riches. Music and song are ways we can praise God's name, but the Word says we can worship God with feasting too (Psalm 22:29). I think that's a great concept! We can worship the Lord with joyful songs (Psalm 100:2). We can worship God with sacrifices and offerings (Isaiah 19:21). We can even worship God by walking and jumping, as the man did who had been lame but now was healed by the name of Jesus (Acts

3:8–9). But regardless of the method, the act of worship must be in spirit (from our rational consciousness) and truth (consistent with the rest of our lives) (John 4:24).

We don't have to be great singers or musicians to worship God. Our worship can be filled with radical demonstrations of praise and other times be very quiet and personal. Neither is better than the other. But we do need to be in a personal relationship with our great God and live with the truth of His greatness reflecting through all we are becoming and all we do.

EXTRAVAGANT WORSHIP IS NOT ACHIEVED BY TAKING SHORTCUTS.

I have lived under the weight of many unhealthy labels in my life, but I have a longing in me for the King of heaven to label me along with Mary as an "extravagant worshiper." As a worship minister, I ask believers to examine themselves and ask, "Are we there yet?" Parents know that phrase is often asked at the beginning of a long, long journey. "Are we there yet? Are we there? Are we there yet?" Even though it seems we've been traveling for hours, we still have a long way to go before our worship will be extravagant.

When the ark of the Lord's covenant was finally brought to its place in the inner sanctuary of the temple, the Most Holy Place, the priests, musicians, and singers joined in unison to bring extravagant worship. "All the Levites who were musicians . . . stood on the east side of the altar, dressed in fine linen and playing cymbals, harps and lyres. They were accompanied by 120 priests sounding trumpets. The trumpeters and singers joined *in unison, as with one voice,* to give praise and thanks to the Lord. Accompanied by trumpets, cymbals and other instruments, they . . . sang: 'He is good; his love endures forever.' Then the temple of the Lord was filled with a cloud, and the priests could not perform their service because of the cloud, for the glory of the Lord filled the temple of God" (2 Chronicles 5:12–14, emphasis added). The priests' attempt to connect with God was blown away by God's coming and connecting with them. Extravagant worship is not achieved by taking shortcuts. People often want quick solutions; they want directions to the easy path; but shortcuts never lead to the gold in life. Most shortcuts eventually become setbacks. I have tried shortcuts to worship, and I have tried to do things my way, but I only ended up frustrated, and the goal I was chasing seemed farther and farther away. To practice extravagant worship, we need to get good at saying, "I lay down my life." Come to Jesus with a grateful heart, and in everything you do live a lifestyle filled with extravagant worship.

Sacrificial Worship Pleases God

Noah was an extravagant worshiper. Genesis 8:20–22 says that after the flood Noah built an altar to the Lord, and taking some of all the clean animals and clean birds, he sacrificed burnt offerings on it. It's hard to fathom the anguish that Noah had to endure. He had just witnessed the incredible drowning of all mankind, while he and his family were saved. He had to shut his ears to the wailing of humanity as he closed the door to the ark God had instructed him to build. Yet he was still obedient to God's instruction to offer a sacrifice of praise when they were on dry land again.

When the Lord smelled the pleasing aroma of Noah's sacrifice, He said in His heart: "Never again will I curse the ground because of man, even though every inclination of his heart is evil from childhood. And never again will I destroy all living creatures, as I have done. As long as the earth endures, seedtime and harvest, cold and heat, summer and winter, day and night will never cease." God gave us a covenant promise that He will not destroy all living creatures again, because of one man who offered extravagant, overgenerous worship in obedience to God's command. Noah lived through extreme circumstances, but he still praised God in the midst of it. That's extravagant worship.

When God tested Abraham, He said, "Take your son, your only son, Isaac, whom you love, and go to the region of Moriah. Sacrifice him there as a burnt offering on one of the mountains I will tell you about" (Genesis 22:2). It's a great challenge to think that God would ask us to place what we love the most on the altar. But Abraham built the altar, then bound his son and laid him on it. He reached out his hand and took up his knife to slay his precious boy. "But the angel of the Lord called out to him from heaven, 'Abraham! Abraham!' 'Here I am,' he replied. 'Do not lay a hand on the boy,' he said. 'Do not do anything to him. Now I know that you fear God, because you have not withheld from me your son, your only son' " (Genesis 22:11–12). Abraham was prepared to give it all. He was overgenerous, excessive in his act of worship. He was prepared to give to the Lord the thing that he loved the most; he passed the big test.

David wanted to offer a sacrifice to the Lord to stop a plague on the Lord's people. So he asked Araunah to sell him a place on his threshing floor to build an altar. Araunah wanted to give the area and livestock needed for David's sacrifice at no charge. But David said, "No, I insist on paying the full price. I will not take for the Lord what is yours, or sacrifice a burnt offering that costs me nothing" (1 Chronicles 21:24).

Extravagant worship grabs God's attention. When Paul and Silas were in jail, they worshiped God. They knew He would never fail them. Even though they had been flogged for preaching the Gospel and now had their feet in stocks, they prayed and sang to God. Suddenly, while they were worshiping, a violent earthquake opened all the doors of the prison. Even with the doors opened, Paul and Silas didn't run. Thinking his prisoners had escaped, the jailer was so distraught that he was about to kill himself, but Paul and Silas stopped him and led him to salvation. Then God moved on the hearts of the magistrates, and they ordered that Paul and Silas be released and go in peace. God supernaturally delivered them from that prison (Acts 16:23–35).

These stories demonstrate that a lifestyle of worship is to live a life of extravagant love for God. Throughout the stories in the Bible, whenever someone demonstrated extravagant worship, God reacted with extravagant blessing. It's cause and effect. Extravagant worship brings extravagant results. What makes worship extravagant? It must cost us something. Worship is an act of obedient faith, even when circumstances offer opportunities to fear. Worship, love, and obedience are tied together.

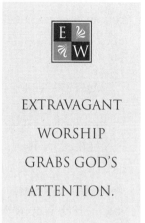

EXTRAVAGANT
WORSHIP
GRABS GOD'S
ATTENTION.

As you seek first the kingdom of God and *obey* the Spirit of God, He calls you on to a greater and deeper knowledge of himself. The first commandment is to love the Lord your God with *all* your heart, with *all* your soul, and with *all* your mind. Jesus said,

> *"Whoever has my commands and obeys them, he is the one who loves me. He who loves me will be loved by my Father, and I too will love him and show myself to him. . . . If anyone loves me, he will obey my teaching. My Father will love him, and we will come to him and make our home with him. He who does not love me will not obey my teaching. These words you hear are not my own; they belong to the Father who sent me" (John 14:21, 23–24).*

Sincerity, integrity, honesty, obedience, and truth are key words to an extravagant worship experience. As worshipers, true lovers of Jesus, we need to be sincere in our worship and to obey and love God with an undivided heart. David prayed, "Give me an undivided heart, that I may fear your name" (Psalm 86:11). He obviously understood that he was an imperfect man, yearning to please a perfect God. David asked for help because his heart had a tendency to stray . . . as does ours. Make this your prayer as you serve God passionately with your life. Ask God to give you a heart that is true and pleasing to Him. Inviting God to give you an undivided heart will open the blessings of heaven to pour out upon your world.

WORSHIP THE AUTHOR OF LOVE

To be a worshiper is to fall in love with God, the Author of love, and accept the love He has for you. He adores you. God gave you His Word as a living love letter that contains everything you will ever need to get through this life and beyond. The Word encourages us to be established in love and to grasp how wide and long and high and deep the love of Christ is for us. His love "surpasses knowledge" (Ephesians 3:19). His love is at work within us, filling us to the measure with the fullness of God. If we could understand even an inkling of this love Christ has for us, our hearts would be full of extravagant worship for the One who loves us so much.

I often try to grasp the depth of this love that is beyond "human knowledge." The many songs I've written to express my love for God don't come close to what I'm trying to say. But I can show the Lord how much I love Him by loving others. I can demonstrate my love for God by living out my part of the Great Commission and bringing the Author of love himself to our love-starved planet. I can determine to love others like He loves.

When I was saved I cried and cried in the presence of God. Tears of gratitude flowed easily as He restored my heart and filled me with His unconditional love. Now all I want to do is sing of His awesome, healing love forever, and I don't care who hears me! I want to tell the world! I will sing of His love until they carry me off in a box—even then I hope I will still be heard humming!

To understand the power of God's love and the power of loving others, go to the Author of love himself and let His letter of love be imprinted on your life.

They will tell of the power of your awesome works, and I will proclaim
your great deeds. They will celebrate your abundant
goodness and joyfully sing of your righteousness.
The Lord is gracious and compassionate, slow to anger and rich in love.
The Lord is good to all; he has compassion on all he has made.
(Psalm 145:6–9)

One of the biggest challenges in life, of the mind and soul, is to accept the love of God—simply to accept God's love for you as a gift. It is the greatest absolute in your life. I wish I could sing the childhood song "Jesus Loves Me" to every human being on earth. If only everyone believed the profound truth in these simple lyrics. Even toddlers can sing the words that continue to set people free: "Yes, Jesus loves me; Yes, Jesus loves me; Yes, Jesus loves me; the Bible tells me so."

"For God so greatly loved and dearly prized the world that He gave His only begotten Son" (John 3:16 AMP).

Many people try to earn love. They try to earn the love of God by working for Him. They find it hard to worship Him because they know they don't deserve His attention. They beat themselves up trying to sub-consciously please Him and earn His grace and favor, without ever truly knowing Him. Nothing you do could make Him love you more.

For he chose us in him before the creation of the world to be holy and
blameless in his sight. In love he predestined us to be adopted as his sons
through Jesus Christ, in accordance with his pleasure and will—to the
praise of his glorious grace, which he has freely given us in the One he
loves. In him we have redemption through his blood, the forgiveness of
sins, in accordance with the riches of God's grace that he lavished
on us with all wisdom and understanding. (Ephesians 1:4–8)

TO YOU

HERE I STAND
FOREVER IN YOUR MIGHTY HAND
LIVING WITH YOUR PROMISE
WRITTEN ON MY HEART
I AM YOURS
SURRENDERED WHOLLY TO YOU
YOU SET ME IN YOUR FAMILY
CALLING ME YOUR OWN
NOW I, I BELONG TO YOU
ALL I NEED
YOUR SPIRIT, YOUR WORD, YOUR TRUTH
HEAR MY CRY, MY DEEP DESIRE
TO KNOW YOU MORE
IN YOUR NAME
I WILL LIFT MY HANDS TO THE KING
THIS ANTHEM OF PRAISE I BRING
HEAVEN KNOWS I LONG TO LOVE YOU
WITH ALL I AM
I BELONG TO YOU

2000 DARLENE ZSCHECH
HILLSONG PUBLISHING

In my song "To You," the lyrics say, "living with Your promise written on my heart." God's Word doesn't just float occasionally into our heads when we need to be pepped up. He writes His love letter on our hearts so that it is always near us when we need His direction and reassurance. Because His love is in our hearts, we have the power to love others.

Dear friends, let us love one another, for love comes from God. Everyone who loves has been born of God and knows God. Whoever does not love does not know God, because God is love. This is how God showed his love among us: He sent his one and only Son into the world that we might live through him. This is love: not that we loved God, but that he loved us and sent his Son as an atoning sacrifice for our sins.
Dear friends, since God so loved us, we also ought to love one another. No one has ever seen God; but if we love one another, God lives in us and his love is made complete in us. We know that we live in him and he in us, because he has given us of his Spirit.
(1 John 4:7–13)

UNTIL YOU KNOW THROUGH PERSONAL EXPERIENCE WHO GOD IS, YOU WILL NEVER TRULY KNOW WHO YOU ARE.

The next few verses in this passage explain that believers love others because God loves us. If people say they love God but hate others, the Word says they are liars. It is not possible to hate people if God is truly within us. Loving others is an act of worship toward the Author of love. People will not understand or grasp how great God is until His disciples show genuine love toward them.

Until you know through personal experience who God is, you will never truly know who you are. And until you know the depth of His love for you, you will never truly experience knowing beyond a shadow of a doubt that you are loved. Until you know that you are loved, you can never obey the second commandment, which is to love others as you love yourself. The Bible continually exhorts us to love one another. Truthful worshipers love God extravagantly and love people with the extravagant love of God.

KNOW YOUR WORTH

Many people, including myself, have battled with insecurity, inadequacy, and intimidation—all the "in" words. But Jesus said,

Do not be afraid of those who kill the body but cannot kill the soul. Rather, be afraid of the One who can destroy both soul and body in hell. Are not two sparrows sold for a penny? Yet not one of them will fall to the ground apart from the will of your Father. And even the very hairs of your head are all numbered. So don't be afraid; you are worth more than many sparrows. Whoever acknowledges me before men, I will also acknowledge him before my Father in heaven. (Matthew 10:28–32)

GOD LOOKS AT US JUST AS A LOVING PARENT LOOKS AT HIS CHILDREN.

It is difficult to carry the weight of inferiority into our time of worship. Worship is a time to focus on who God is; it is a time to enjoy the awesome authority and anointing that He puts on His people who come into His presence with praise. Sometimes the Enemy works very hard to keep us from worshiping freely, but sometimes we simply lack discipline in our thought life.

If we read the Word and keep God's truth in our heart, we will focus our attention on His greatness and on the value that He places on us. "Don't be afraid," He said, "you are worth more than many sparrows." I love those words. Knowing our value enriches our worship of God, and not because of what we do, but because of who He is. God sees all of our inadequacies through the blood of Christ. Because of Jesus, our heavenly Father sees us just as He sees His Son—beautiful and perfect.

God looks at us just as a loving parent looks at his children. My three daughters could be naughty; but I look at them, and I think they are perfect. They are totally luscious! Unapologetically, I think they are magnificent. I think the day God put them on the earth He did the best thing He has ever done! That is the heart of a parent, and how much more does God look at us and say, "Oh, they are my precious, beloved children."

When we do mess up, Jesus stands as our high priest before the Father to defend us. He tells the Father, "They are the ones you have given me. I am in them, and you are in me. Look at how beautiful they are." Because of Jesus, we can "approach the throne of grace with confidence, so that we may receive mercy and find grace to help us in our time of need" (Hebrews 4:16). That should give us enough courage to stand up straight and understand our value; not because of who we are or anything we have ever done; we are valuable because Jesus loves us.

When you understand who you are in Christ, a rest enters your soul that cannot coexist with striving and struggling. Just as darkness cannot coexist with light, striving for approval does not coexist with confidence in His grace. Who you are in Christ matters more than what you do. God accepts and

WHEN YOU UNDERSTAND WHO YOU ARE IN CHRIST, A REST ENTERS YOUR SOUL THAT CANNOT COEXIST WITH STRIVING AND STRUGGLING.

loves you, just as you are, to demonstrate His glory to all the world.

First Corinthians 1:26–31 says,

Think of what you were when you were called. Not many of you were wise by human standards; not many were influential; not many were of noble birth. But God chose the foolish things of the world to shame the wise; God chose the weak things of the world to shame the strong. He chose the lowly things of this world and the despised things—and the things that are not—to nullify the things that are, so that no one may boast before him. It is because of him that you are in Christ Jesus, who has become for us wisdom from God—that is, our righteousness, holiness and redemption. Therefore, as it is written: "Let him who boasts boast in the Lord."

That's my testimony; I was the girl "least likely to succeed." The first ministry trip my husband and I went on with our senior pastor, Brian Houston, was to England. I sang a song with a backup soundtrack before Pastor Brian preached. I found out that one of the pastors in the church we ministered in said to Brian, "You were fantastic, but she doesn't have what it takes." But God has given me opportunities beyond my hopes or imaginations.

My future has never relied on anyone else's opinion of my ability. I'm a testimony of God's grace. God uses people who say, "Well, Lord, this is all I have to offer you; so if I'm going to be used in the kingdom, *you* will have to work through me." The very least we can do is give God our lives and let Him show us the great things He can do through our yielded hearts and hands.

We have been created with the divine purpose of having Jesus as the center of our existence. We were created to worship Him in all we do.

Therefore, brothers, since we have confidence to enter the Most Holy Place by the blood of Jesus, by a new and living way opened for us through the curtain, that is, his body, and since we have a great priest over the house of God, let us draw near to God with a sincere heart in

full assurance of faith, having our hearts sprinkled to cleanse us from a
guilty conscience and having our bodies washed with pure water.
Let us hold unswervingly to the hope we profess,
for he who promised is faithful. (Hebrews 10:19–23)

We have an invitation to enter into the Most Holy Place, where our heavenly Father sits. Through worship we put Christ as the chief corner-stone of our lives, and the power we have access to in His presence is real. He longs for us to draw closer to Him. He has cleansed our hearts and made them pure so that we can stand in His presence. So we continue to praise our mighty Lord—to sing, clap, dance, celebrate, get soaked in His presence and overwhelmed by His grace.

Shout for joy to the Lord. . . . Worship the Lord with gladness; come
before him with joyful songs. Know that the Lord is God. It is he who
made us, and we are his; we are his people, the sheep of his pasture.
Enter his gates with thanksgiving and his courts with praise; give thanks
to him and praise his name. For the Lord is good and his love
endures forever; his faithfulness continues through all generations.
(Psalm 100:1–5)

DEVOTE YOURSELF TO PRAYER AND MEDITATION

Extravagant worshipers know the power of seeking God through prayer and meditation. The Word says, "Devote yourselves to prayer" (1 Corinthians 7:5). And meditate on the Word "day and night, so that you may be careful to do everything written in it. Then you will be prosperous and successful" (Joshua 1:8). God's Word is so clear: "Rejoice always, pray without ceasing, in everything give thanks; for this is the will of God in Christ Jesus for you" (1 Thessalonians 5:16–18).

Rejoice, pray, and be thankful. As worshipers, we seek the face of the Almighty King. We seek His face more than we seek any gifts or accolades. When reading through the lives of Bible heroes such as Abraham, Joseph, and Moses, one can see that they were not perfect men; but they continually fellowshiped with God and worshiped Him. They were openly thankful for what God did for them, and their worship of the Lord flowed from a natural response to their relationship with Him.

People have accused me of a performance-based ministry, of being too expressive, but there is a fire in my inmost being that I can't contain. God's love and forgiveness and the power of the cross cause me to dance into my future, regardless of what people think. And hey, what can I say . . . I am a woman in love! When I joined my first worship team in my mid-teens, I tried hard to participate in what I thought was worship. I became boring—not extravagant. It was in my thinking that to be a Christian musician meant mediocre, nothing extreme, quiet and safe, as if somehow this conformity made me more holy. But only a few years ago I decided to be all that God predestined me to be. Bland doesn't mean righteous, and I had permission from the King to let "all that is within me bless His holy name" (Psalm 103:1 KJV).

When King David brought the ark of the covenant (representing the presence of God) into the city, he danced and celebrated amid the joyful singing, shouts, the sounding of rams' horns, trumpets, cymbals, lyres, and harps. Triumphant praise resounded as all of Israel joined in the thanksgiving parade! David's worship was so extravagant that his wife, Michal, felt he was making a fool of himself. From that day she despised him in her heart. If David's worship had been halfhearted, Michal would not have reacted so strongly to him. Casual worship wouldn't have disturbed Michal, but David was radical in his expression of worship that day. David had extravagant love for the Lord, and he praised his Lord with reckless abandon! He was crazy with enthusiasm because he was so in love with God.

When we are extravagantly worshiping God, we may have onlookers who won't respond the way we'd hoped. Someone may watch us as we lay down our lives to worship our Lord. The testimony of our adoration may be viewed as something of great value that will cause others to join in, but it may also make someone despise us for the freedom and the joy that we are living in. But worship is unto the Lord and not unto men. Worship is an act of seeking God's face and enjoying His magnificent presence.

David's psalm of thanksgiving in 1 Chronicles 16:7–36 narrates the depth and magnitude of high praise and truthful worship. David said, "Sing to him, sing praise to him; tell of all his wonderful acts. Glory in his holy name; let the hearts of those who seek the Lord rejoice. Look to the Lord and his strength; seek his face always."

I encourage you to diligently seek the Lord and to love Him with all your heart. Learn to seek God's face without worrying about saving yours. Know how to get on your knees. Don't worry if you don't look cool in worship. If your heart is full of radical praise, then be truthful in your expression of love toward Him; release your extravagant worship.

"My soul longs, yes, even faints for the courts of the Lord; My heart and my flesh cry out for the living God" (Psalm 84:2). Is that how your heart beats for Him? Be radical in your pursuit of Christ. Your worship offering to Him will bless His heart as He hears you crying out for more of Him. Be filled to overflowing in your zeal for God as you continue to build your relationship with Him through His Word. Worship Him with a heart that longs to be with Him. As you bring a heart hungry to know Him more and express through music and song your desire to love Him more, the possibilities are limitless.

What Can I Bring to the Altar?

One thing that can stop us from being a truthful worshiper is feeling like we have nothing to offer to God. The Bible says, "Bring an offering; bring an offering; bring an offering," and feeling empty-handed with nothing to contribute to the relationship with God can stop us from plunging boldly into worship. But when Christ came into the world, He showed us that God only wants something that we do have to give to Him. He said that sacrifices, burnt offerings, and sin offerings did not please God. Then He said, "Here I am—it is written about me in the scroll—I have come to do your will, O God" (Hebrews 10:5–7).

The only thing God wants from you is your heart. God says, "I don't need your talent. I don't need your gift. I don't want all the stuff that you can do. I just want *you*. I want your heart." David was the runt of the litter, overlooked as the one nobody wanted, but God loved his heart. He said, "I have found David son of Jesse a man after my own heart; he will do everything I want him to do" (Acts 13:22). God saw David's heart and ready obedience, and He responded to David's offering in a magnificent way—He made him king over His chosen people.

One morning I was lying in bed, when Chloe said, "Mummy, sit up, sit up; I want to make you breakfast." She was five at the time, so I knew her meal would be unique! She knew I liked toast, but she's not allowed to use the toaster, and we keep the bread in the freezer. So her "toast" was rock hard. I also drink herbal tea, but she's not allowed to use the kettle, so she put a teabag in a cup with cold water. And I don't know where it came from, but she added a squashed banana to my breakfast tray.

She was so proud of herself when she put the tray on my lap. Words failed me.

"Do you love it, Mum?"

"Yep, I sure do!" I waited for her to leave, but she didn't. "Thank you, Chloe, this is lovely." She sat on my bed, looked at me with the cutest expression, and waited. Suddenly I knew that *I had to eat the breakfast!*

"Mmmmm, Chloe, it's beautiful!" The look on her face was priceless. She didn't bring me breakfast to win points with me. She was too young yet to know that there might be money attached. All she wanted to do was to bless me. She gave me her best with a pure heart.

You are not empty-handed, with nothing to bring to the table. God doesn't want what you are going to be or what you would like to be. He wants all that you are today. You can offer yourself to Him in worship; you can let that explosion of faith force you to praise His name and offer your attention to bless Him. Do you think giving your heart will bless God? Chloe blessed me. I still talk about it! And you will bless God, because He looks past all the stuff of life and looks straight to the heart.

When I exalt the Lord, God is increased, and the "me" in my life is decreased! I know I need more of God and less of me. I need more of His wisdom and less of my great ideas. I need more of His presence and less of my talent. Isn't that what we all need?

When we worship God, He is exalted, and our problems shrivel in His presence. "Turn your eyes upon Jesus, look full in His wonderful face. And the things of earth will grow strangely dim in the light of His glory and grace." Remember that song? That is the truth. When He is exalted, everything about us—the good, the bad, and the ugly—is decreased as we focus on Him.

IT IS YOU

LAMP UNTO MY FEET
LIGHT UNTO MY PATH
IT IS YOU, JESUS, IT IS YOU
THIS TREASURE THAT I HOLD
MORE THAN FINEST GOLD
IT IS YOU, JESUS, IT IS YOU
WITH ALL MY HEART
WITH ALL MY SOUL
I LIVE TO WORSHIP YOU
AND PRAISE FOREVER MORE
PRAISE FOREVER MORE
LORD, EVERY DAY
I NEED YOU MORE
ON WINGS OF HEAVEN I WILL SOAR
WITH YOU
YOU TAKE MY BROKENNESS
CALL ME TO YOURSELF
THERE YOU STAND
HEALING IN YOUR HANDS

1999 DARLENE ZSCHECH
HILLSONG PUBLISHING

Chapter Two

EXPLOSIVE
PRAISE

EXPLOSIVE PRAISE

W hen Jehoshaphat learned that a vast army from three nations was coming against him, he did what any extravagant worshiper would do. He called the people of Judah together to unite in worship and praise to God, saying,

> *O Lord, God of our fathers, are you not the God who is in heaven? You rule over all the kingdoms of the nations. Power and might are in your hand, and no one can withstand you.*
> *O our God, did you not drive out the inhabitants of this land before your people Israel and give it forever to the descendants of Abraham your friend? They have lived in it and have built in it a sanctuary for your Name, saying, "If calamity comes upon us, whether the sword of judgment, or plague or famine, we will stand in your presence before this temple that bears your Name and will cry out to you in our distress, and you will hear us and save us"*
> *(2 Chronicles 20:2–9).*

Before placing his army in positions of defense, Jehoshaphat "appointed men to sing to the Lord and to praise him for the splendor of his holiness as they went out at the head of the army, saying, 'Give thanks to the Lord, for his love endures forever' " (v. 21). When Jehoshaphat and his team marched forward to slay their enemies, they went singing and praising God with thanksgiving for His enduring love. As the people of Judah sang praises to the Lord, the enemy armies attacked each other until every last soldier was dead. The Lord set ambushes against the enemy, and the battle was won!

"So Jehoshaphat and his men went to carry off their plunder, and they found among them a great amount of equipment and clothing and also articles of value—more than they could take away. There was so much plunder that it took three days to collect it [v. 25]. The fear of God came upon all the kingdoms of the countries when they heard how the Lord had fought against the enemies of Israel [v. 29]." There was great rejoicing, great blessing, and an even greater testimony to the power of God among all the people!

WHEN WE, GOD'S PEOPLE, COME INTO HIS PRESENCE WITH THANKS- GIVING AND PRAISE, WARFARE IS WAGED AGAINST OUR ENEMIES.

When we, God's people, come into His presence with thanksgiving and praise, warfare is waged against our enemies, and our battles are won by the supernatural power of God. In the face of challenge and persecution, God's people are to unite and praise Him. The Enemy has no chance of winning against people who are consumed with praising God. There is no victory against those who rejoice in God's great glory.

I used to joke with my worship team that the reason Jehoshaphat's enemy was defeated was because the singers and musicians were so bad—perhaps it was more like torture! Their enemies conceded quickly, saying, "Okay, you win, we give up; just stop the singing!" But even if the people *were* tone deaf and couldn't carry a musical note, the Lord would have eagerly received their praises. It wasn't the harmony that defeated their enemy; it was the presence of God's mighty power that warred on their behalf and won their battles.

Praise is not a "happy-clappy" song. Praise is not the fast songs before the nice, slow worship songs. Praise is a declaration, a victory cry, proclaiming faith to stand firm in the place God has given you. Praise is a proclamation that the Enemy's intent to plunder you will not rock you.

Praise declares that you will not be moved by the Enemy's attempt to snatch you away.

If you need to have the Enemy flee from your life, then you need to praise your pathway to victory! Praising God with other believers releases explosive faith that frightens the Enemy. This time of high praise, when we have broken away from self-concerns and when we are truly rejoicing in our Lord, is confronting; and you cannot stay in your comfort zone if you want to enter in. Praise is a powerful war cry declaring that you will stand strong and you will praise God at all times through all circumstances. Praise takes you into the presence of God where the Enemy has no choice but to flee. I call praise an explosion of faith that allows you to run straight into the loving arms of Jesus. Praise extends beyond what you feel, how your week has been, how your day has been, whether you have much or little. It allows you to go straight to the magnificent reality of Christ, our glorious Lord and King of Kings.

A number of years ago during a trip to South Africa, I visited an orphanage and AIDS hospital, which was filled to overflowing with extremely sick, abandoned kids. It was heartbreaking to see so many gorgeous children, all created with destiny and purpose, so sick. Most had been left in gutters to fend for themselves. These places of refuge where I saw them were supported by a local

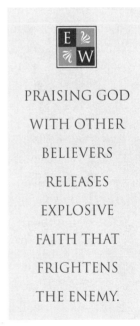

PRAISING GOD WITH OTHER BELIEVERS RELEASES EXPLOSIVE FAITH THAT FRIGHTENS THE ENEMY.

church and staffed by Spirit-filled believers, who led every single child in their care into a divine relationship with Jesus. In a ward where only chronically ill AIDS patients were, a precious young girl handed me the following letter:

What you are doing is what our Father wants you to do, Miss Darlene, so do what you do in your very best, and may God bless you more and more . . . and we thank Him for everything and we know Him.

God Bless you, Miss Darlene.

Then fifteen of the older kids came into the little sitting room and sang the song "All Things Are Possible" for me. I was a mess, but they were radiant and genuinely glad. They put the reality of Christ ahead of their AIDS-riddled bodies. They sang with such faith!

Three months later all the children in the AIDS hospital that I had met that day had gone to be with Jesus. Their lives and the praise they had for God gave us a new perspective of our own lives. We are easily distracted by things that don't really matter. The memory of those children remind me to serve the Lord with gladness, praising Christ, for *in Him* we live, *in Him* we move, and *in Him* we have our being.

GOD INHABITS OUR PRAISES

The Word says that God *inhabits* the praises of His people (Psalm 22:3). It's amazing to think that God, in all His fullness, inhabits and dwells in *our* praises of Him. When someone asks, "Where is God in this situation?" we know that God is found in our praises. He occupies our praise, and with His presence He brings His love, His healing, His forgiveness, His grace, and His mercy. Whatever is needed to make a situation turn around for the good is present as we praise the Lord.

God inhabits your praises—not just my praises—not just on Sunday in church, but at your home, while you're at work, and when you're washing clothes or preparing a meal for friends and family. God, in all His fullness, inhabits your praises. If you could grasp this truth, you would understand that every time you praise Him, every time you worship Him, He is present to meet your needs. As you praise and worship Him, name your needs, and watch Jesus answer your need. He is all you need.

ALL THINGS ARE POSSIBLE

ALMIGHTY GOD, MY REDEEMER
MY HIDING PLACE, MY SAFE REFUGE
NO OTHER NAME LIKE JESUS
NO POWER CAN STAND AGAINST YOU
MY FEET ARE PLANTED ON THIS ROCK
AND I WILL NOT BE SHAKEN
MY HOPE, IT COMES FROM YOU ALONE
MY LORD AND MY SALVATION
YOUR PRAISE IS ALWAYS ON MY LIPS
YOUR WORD IS LIVING IN MY HEART
AND I WILL PRAISE YOU WITH A NEW SONG
MY SOUL WILL BLESS YOU, LORD
YOU FILL MY LIFE WITH GREATER JOY
YES, I DELIGHT MYSELF IN YOU
AND I WILL PRAISE YOU WITH A NEW SONG
MY SOUL WILL BLESS YOU, LORD
WHEN I AM WEAK, YOU MAKE ME STRONG
WHEN I'M POOR, I KNOW I'M RICH
FOR IN THE POWER OF YOUR NAME
ALL THINGS ARE POSSIBLE.

1997 DARLENE ZSCHECH
HILLSONG PUBLISHING

I visited a church once where the members wouldn't sing the song "Jesus, You're All I Need." They said they didn't agree with it. They were thinking on a practical level: they needed food, they needed air to breathe, etc. But without Jesus we actually don't need anything else, because without Jesus life is not worth living. I need Jesus. You need Jesus. He is *all* we need.

Our praise is irresistible to God. As soon as He hears us call His name, He is ready to answer us. That is the God we serve. Every time the praise and worship teams with our musicians, singers, production teams, dancers, and actors begin to praise God, His presence comes in like a flood. Even though we live in His presence, His love is *lavished* on us in a miraculous way when we praise Him!

THE POWER OF PRAISE

Praise and worship breaks through all boundaries of talent and ability. Praise *invades hell and excites heaven*! When we praise God, we must think beyond notes, form, or technique. Praise and worship is a

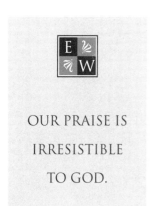

OUR PRAISE IS IRRESISTIBLE TO GOD.

powerful expression of love that transcends the possibilities of music. It is given to us as a weapon of warfare or as a warm blanket on a cold night. Praise is a supernatural way of expressing our thanks to our ever-loving God.

We must never underestimate the gift and the power of praise and worship. As we obediently bring to Him the little we can offer Him through praise, He is *always* faithful to respond with the greatness He has to return.

As we grasp this weapon of praise God has given us to advance the kingdom, we should ready ourselves for the countless miraculous, supernatural moments in our lives.

Psalm 8:2 says, "From the lips of children and infants you have ordained praise because of your enemies, to silence the foe and the avenger." This verse tells us that even our babies have been ordained by the Lord Most High to silence the Enemy with praise. Silence the foe and rebuke the avenger with your praise! When you sing, praise, dance, and rejoice in the face of opposition, you are using the spiritual warfare weapons against the devil. Paul describes this in 2 Corinthians 10:4, when he says, "The weapons we fight with are not the weapons of the world. On the contrary, they have divine power to demolish strongholds."

In May 2000 we were preparing to go on a three-week Hillsong worship tour through the USA. These tours are intense both spiritually and physically, but the miracles we see happen through them are incredible. I was twelve weeks pregnant with a child we had planned for and waited on for a very long time. Three days before we were to leave, Mark and I went to the obstetrician and found out that the baby had just died in my womb.

I was shattered and brokenhearted; the agony of that moment was indescribable. It was an awful and terrible loss. We had taken separate cars to the doctor, so I had to drive back to the house by myself with Mark following me. I got in the car, and I just didn't know what to think or do. I felt the depth of my sadness would become too heavy to bear. Then I heard the Holy Spirit whisper, *"Sing."*

In that moment it was the absolute last thing I wanted to do. *Sing?* I couldn't think of anything that I felt less like doing. But again I heard the Holy Spirit say, *"Sing."* So after years of learning it is much better to obey quickly, I started to sing. My head didn't sing, and I do not even know if my heart sang, but my soul sang. It was almost involuntary. I sang two songs. The first song that I heard coming out of my mouth was the hymn "Then sings my soul, my Savior God to thee, how great thou art . . . ," which really surprised me, as this was a song we sang at my father's

HOW GREAT THOU ART

O LORD MY GOD,
WHEN I IN AWESOME WONDER
CONSIDER ALL THE WORLDS
THY HANDS HAVE MADE
I SEE THE STARS,
I HEAR THE ROLLING THUNDER,
THY POWER THROUGHOUT
THE UNIVERSE DISPLAYED!
THEN SINGS MY SOUL,
MY SAVIOR GOD TO THEE,
HOW GREAT THOU ART,
HOW GREAT THOU ART!

1953 STUART K. HINE
KINGSWAY THANKYOU MUSIC*

funeral. The lyrics are about putting the Word of God above anything we could be humanly facing and being triumphant in Him. The second song was one I had written years before called "I Will Bless You, Lord." The chorus says, "How my soul cries out to You, O God. I will bless You, Lord." Again, even though my thoughts were full of despair, the core of my being, my soul, was singing rather than my intellect.

By the time I got home something had definitely transpired in the spiritual realm. I had spoken many times on the power of worshiping through a trial. I had done this myself in varying degrees, but never before had I experienced the power of God so sovereignly fulfilling His promise to "heal the brokenhearted and bind up their wounds" (Psalm 147:3). The sweet presence of our glorious Savior placed me on the way to personal healing and victory.

I still had to go through the physical ramifications of losing a child, the operation, telling our girls, telling our church family, who had been so excited for us, and hours and hours of tears. But Mark and I made the decision to continue with our plans and go on the worship tour. It was probably one of the hardest things I have ever done. But again, night after night I found myself saturated in His presence as I led worship from a position of faith. I chose to lead worship and not give the Enemy any more ground than he had already taken. I continued in a daily decision to lift my eyes and praise Him with all I had. I found my

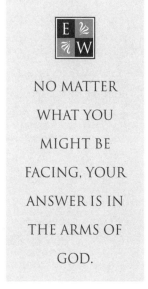

NO MATTER WHAT YOU MIGHT BE FACING, YOUR ANSWER IS IN THE ARMS OF GOD.

healing in the arms of God, and even though grief still took its natural course, I found the truth of "Sing, oh, barren woman . . ." I will always treasure and thank God for the child I carried only twelve weeks.

No matter what you might be facing, your answer is in the arms of

God. Psalm 138:2 says, "I will bow down toward your holy temple and will praise your name for your love and your faithfulness, for you have exalted above all things your name and your word." This is a powerful Scripture. He is exalted above anything that you face—above any disappointment, above any brokenness, above anything that tries to exalt itself higher than the name of Jesus. He has promised us His Name and His Word. Psalm 138:3 says, "When I called, you answered me; you made me bold and stouthearted." *Stouthearted* means courageous. God makes His people a brave company of men and women.

ENTER HIS GATES WITH THANKSGIVING

Enter his gates with thanksgiving and his courts with praise;
give thanks to him and praise his name (Psalm 100:4).

To mindlessly go through the motions of praising God without purposefully entering His gates with the grandest of thanksgiving is like holding on to a grenade without ever taking out the pin or owning a painting by Leonardo da Vinci and keeping it in safe storage. I have even heard praise songs referred to as the "appetizers" or the "cocktails" of the worship service! To reduce "earth-shattering victory cries" to statements such as these must sadden God's heart as He patiently waits again for us to walk in the power of His promises. "He who sacrifices thank offerings honors me, and he prepares the way so that I may show him the salvation of God" (Psalm 50:23).

A powerful truth that our worship team at Hillsong Church has come to understand is that there is a tremendous power in bringing an offering of thanksgiving to God. Philippians 4:6 says, "Do not be anxious about anything, but in everything, by prayer and petition, with thanksgiving, present your requests to God." As worshipers, we are a people who know the power of thanksgiving and who welcome His peace. The Bible says we can enter His gates and His throne and His courts with thanksgiving. It is a powerful opportunity. Thanksgiving paves a way for us to go straight into that awesome throne room of the King of Kings. When you enter into praise with true thanksgiving, the peace of God, which passes all understanding, accompanies your thankful heart.

Praise and worship is prayer. It is intimate; it is intercessory; and it is powerful. After we present our requests to God with thanksgiving, the Word says, "And the peace of God, which transcends all understanding, will guard your hearts and your minds in Christ Jesus" (Philippians 4:7). Explosive praise is about understanding the power of bringing thanksgiving into your worship.

There is a woman in our choir who has every reason to be bitter. Her husband left her when she was pregnant with their fourth child. But she sings in the choir morning, noon, and night and praises God. She has made a way to fulfill the call of God on her life. Her children are thriving; her household is thriving; and she is a testimony to the awesome greatness of God. She has every excuse to stay home, but she is consumed with a passion for her Lord. She could sit at home and feel sorry for herself, but day in and day out she makes a decision to be full of explosive praise.

Give thanks to the Lord, for he is good; his love endures forever.
Let Israel say: "His love endures forever. . . ."
In my anguish I cried to the Lord, and he answered by setting me free.
The Lord is with me; I will not be afraid. What can man do to me? The
Lord is with me; he is my helper. I will look in triumph on my enemies. It
is better to take refuge in the Lord than to trust in man. It is better to
take refuge in the Lord than to trust in princes. All the nations
surrounded me, but in the name of the Lord I cut them off. They
surrounded me on every side, but in the name of the Lord I cut them off.
They swarmed around me like bees, but they died out as quickly as
burning thorns; in the name of the Lord I cut them off. I was pushed

*back and about to fall, but the Lord helped me. The Lord is my strength
and my song; he has become my salvation. Shouts of joy and victory
resound in the tents of the righteous: "The Lord's right hand has done
mighty things! The Lord's right hand is lifted high; the Lord's right hand
has done mighty things!" I will not die but live, and will proclaim what
the Lord has done. . . . The stone the builders rejected has become the
capstone; the Lord has done this, and it is marvelous in our eyes.*
(Psalm 118:1–23)

Jesus faced a gruesome trial, but He still worshiped God with explosive praise. I can imagine Jesus singing Psalm 118 after the Passover meal as He anticipated His crucifixion. Perhaps He sang it moments before He took on the transgressions of humanity so we could be free. Understand the power of explosive praise when you are facing a trial and be tenacious in your praise when you face difficulties.

I love thinking about the life of David because he was an extravagant worshiper who knew the power of explosive praise. David was extravagant when he was good and extravagant when he was bad! But he knew the power of worshiping in the midst of a trial. David was in a bad situation when he wrote the following psalm:

*My enemies say of me in malice, "When will he die and his name
perish?" All my enemies whisper together against me; they imagine the
worst for me, saying, "A vile disease has beset him; he will never get up
from the place where he lies." Even my close friend, whom I trusted, he
who shared my bread, has lifted up his heel against me. But you, O
Lord, have mercy on me; raise me up, that I may repay them. I know
that you are pleased with me, for my enemy does not triumph over me.
In my integrity you uphold me and set me in your presence forever.
Praise be to the Lord, the God of Israel, from everlasting to everlasting.
Amen and Amen. (Psalm 41:5–13)*

David committed adultery and then plotted a man's death. God was not pleased with David. In 2 Samuel 12:13, it says that David repented, and Nathan told him, "The Lord has taken away your sin. You are not going to die." Through God's forgiveness, David was able to stand and say, "In my integrity you uphold me." David understood the power of praising and worshiping God when his world was falling apart. He understood the power of forgiveness, and so he sang of his love for the Lord who would deliver him.

THE POWER OF A SHOUT

The Word of God says, "Come, let us sing for joy to the Lord; let us shout aloud to the Rock of our salvation" (Psalm 95:1). There is great power in a shout. A shout commands attention. A shout is prophetic and faith building; a shout calls things that are not as though they were. A shout demonstrates enthusiasm, confidence, and determination. A shout releases energy, boldness, and passion. A shout changes the atmosphere.

God's Word tells us to shout. "Shout to God with the voice of triumph and songs of joy!" (Psalm 47:1). "Shout for joy" (Psalm 98:4). Isaiah 26:19 says, "Wake up and shout." It doesn't say wake up and shout at your partner. It doesn't say wake up and shout at your kids. It does say to wake up and shout for joy!

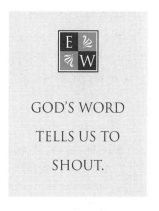

GOD'S WORD TELLS US TO SHOUT.

When I am leading worship, I don't shout to get people excited or "hyped up." When I shout, I am encouraging people to put action to their faith. A shout of joy changes the atmosphere over our lives. Praise is not an angry shout; it's a faith-filled shout! I am a singing teacher's worst nightmare because I strain my voice continually before I start singing. I get excited in the prayer meeting as we lay hold of God and shout His praises!

I want to go into every service full of expectation to see people's lives

SHOUT TO THE LORD

MY JESUS, MY SAVIOR
LORD, THERE IS NONE LIKE YOU
ALL OF MY DAYS, I WANT TO PRAISE
THE WONDERS OF YOUR MIGHTY LOVE
MY COMFORT, MY SHELTER
TOWER OF REFUGE AND STRENGTH
LET EVERY BREATH, ALL THAT I AM
NEVER CEASE TO WORSHIP YOU
SHOUT TO THE LORD
ALL THE EARTH LET US SING
POWER AND MAJESTY
PRAISE TO THE KING
MOUNTAINS BOW DOWN
AND THE SEAS WILL ROAR
AT THE SOUND OF YOUR NAME
I SING FOR JOY
AT THE WORK OF YOUR HANDS
FOREVER I'LL LOVE YOU
FOREVER I'LL STAND
NOTHING COMPARES TO THE PROMISE
I HAVE IN YOU

1993 DARLENE ZSCHECH
HILLSONG PUBLISHING

changed to reflect His grace in their lives. I want people to sing a new song. I want those who are sad to learn to shout! I want those who are timid to shout for joy. I want to help people see the Father, help them to "taste and see that the Lord is good." That is the power of a shout. I want everyone to know the power of a shout to the Lord.

"The Lord their God is with them; the shout of the King is among them" (Numbers 23:21).

The Walls Are Tumbling Down

Walls are spoken of throughout much of the Old Testament. Walls warded off assassins and protected citizens in a safe area. Some walls were so thick that entire communities were built on top of them. People lived on top of the walls so that they could see anything coming, friendly or unfriendly. Emotional walls that were built to protect and enclose them surround many believers. But too often walls that are built for safety become so confining that they do not allow the inner man to be challenged, stretched, or confronted. Some walls were intentionally built to divide and separate people from other believers.

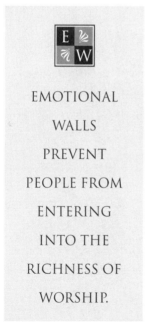

EMOTIONAL WALLS PREVENT PEOPLE FROM ENTERING INTO THE RICHNESS OF WORSHIP.

Emotional walls prevent people from entering into the richness of worship. Instead of protecting us, emotional walls often become strongholds that will eventually destroy us. But the anointing of God pulls down strongholds and breaks the yoke that binds. The name of Jesus pulls down walls. As we lift up His name in worship and praise and let our hearts sing to our Maker, we will see confining walls in our lives come tumbling down. Some walls may be very fragile and easily dismantled, while others may need to be attacked with a shout of praise. Some of our walls may be so thick that they need dynamite to see them smashed.

Some emotional walls are constructed so that inflicted pain can be at a guaranteed minimum or so that love can be received with a minimum of risk. Actually, most walls keep the inner man from receiving any love at all. But the church is being restored, and these walls are breaking and tumbling down through praise and worship. We are being restored as a strong church, full of righteousness, peace, and joy in the Holy Ghost. Shout for joy, because the walls are coming down!

A shout of joy is like a prophetic cry to break obstacles in your life. A shout of praise that comes from the core of who you are and that believes in the divinity and the sovereignty of our God will reap a harvest blessing. God can break through any size wall in your life. He has done so for me time and time again. I've personally seen my own walls of insecurity, pride, mistrust, and fear crumble as I've praised Him!

Shout with joy to God, all the earth! Sing the glory of his name; make his praise glorious! Say to God, "How awesome are your deeds! So great is your power that your enemies cringe before you. All the earth bows down to you; they sing praise to you, they sing praise to your name.
(Psalm 66:1–4).

I love the writings of T. D. Jakes and his wife, Serita. In her book *The Princess Within* (Bethany House Publishers, 2001) Serita writes of Jesus, her Secret Keeper,

> When I came to the realization that the Secret Keeper had already forgiven what I could not forget and that He had already forgotten what I still regretted, there was such a release. The walls I had built to protect my feelings and to hide the guilt of the past became less and less needful. All along I felt I was keeping people from getting in, but in actuality I was prohibiting myself from getting out. An invisible wall trapped me.

That is what happens when you put up walls. You think you are protecting yourself from getting hurt, but you are actually keeping yourself from getting out.

> *In that day you will say: "I will praise you, O Lord. Although you were angry with me, your anger has turned away and you have comforted me. Surely God is my salvation; I will trust and not be afraid. The Lord, the Lord, is my strength and my song; he has become my salvation."*
> *With joy you will draw water from the wells of salvation.*
> *In that day you will say: "Give thanks to the Lord, call on his name; make known among the nations what he has done, and proclaim that his name is exalted. Sing to the Lord, for he has done glorious things; let this be known to all the world. Shout aloud and sing for joy, people of Zion, for great is the Holy One of Israel among you"*
> *(Isaiah 12:1–6).*

I love that God's Word tells us to shout aloud and sing for joy. Every service I start, I shout something like "Welcome to church! Awesome! God is great and greatly to be praised, and we are going to sing His praises! We don't want you to focus on what has been going on in your life, we want you to focus on Jesus and let Him be the answer to every need. Amen! Get on your feet! Clap your hands! Sing His praise! Great is God among us; it is the promise of heaven."

TENACIOUS PRAISE

Be tenacious in your praise and worship, especially when you are facing a trial. Joshua learned the power of tenacious praise when it was time for him to enter the Promised Land. But before God's people could completely move in, the wall that surrounded the fortified city of Jericho needed to come tumbling down. And this was a wall with people living on it.

In Joshua 1:2–5, the Lord spoke to Joshua and said,

Moses my servant is dead. Now then, you and all these people, get ready to cross the Jordan River into the land I am about to give to them—to the Israelites. I will give you every place where you set your foot, as I promised Moses. . . . No one will be able to stand up against you all the days of your life. As I was with Moses, so I will be with you; I will never leave you nor forsake you.

Joshua had been instructed to break the wall and to take possession of the Promised Land. The Lord said to Joshua (vv. 6–8),

Be strong and courageous, because you will lead these people to inherit the land I swore to their forefathers to give them. Be strong and very courageous. Be careful to obey all the law my servant Moses gave you; do not turn from it to the right or to the left, that you may be successful wherever you go. Do not let this Book of the Law depart from your mouth; meditate on it day and night, so that you may be careful to do everything written in it. Then you will be prosperous and successful.

I would have been nervous if God had only asked me twice to be courageous. But just as the Lord kept telling Joshua to be strong and courageous, He is telling you not to be discouraged, because the Lord your God will be with you wherever you go. The Promised Land is on the other side of your emotional wall. What is your wall?

If you are going to attack your wall, then you need to have the Word of the Lord hidden and firmly established in your heart. Joshua had the Word of the Lord and nothing else with which to fight. He had the Word of the Lord and a very big wall!

In Joshua 2:9–11, we read about Rahab, the prostitute living on the wall of Jericho, who hid Joshua when he was spying on the land. She said to him,

I know that the Lord has given this land to you and that a great fear of you has fallen on us, so that all who live in this country are melting in fear because of you. We have heard how the Lord dried up the water of

the Red Sea for you when you came out of Egypt, and what you did to
Sihon and Og, the two kings of the Amorites east of the Jordan, whom
you completely destroyed. When we heard of it, our hearts melted and
everyone's courage failed because of you, for the Lord your God
is God in heaven above and on the earth below.

Joshua must have been filled with courage when he learned that the hearts of his enemies were melting with fear. When Joshua readied his army and moved into position to march around the city as God had instructed him to do, the enemy's camp got nervous. Not because Joshua was brilliant, but because they had heard about the power of his God. Isn't that great?!

When you step out in tenacious courage to attack the walls in your life, you will make the devil nervous too. When you bring an extravagant offering of worship to God, when you give a mighty victory cry of praise, the devil gets nervous because he knows the power of our God to pull down strongholds that keep us bound. He knows that we will be free as soon as we "shout to the Lord in worship and praise."

After Joshua had prepared all that God had told him to do, he advanced toward his wall. Joshua 6:6–7 says that he was to take up the ark of the covenant of the Lord (the presence of God) and make seven priests carry trumpets of rams' horns in front of the ark (this is when the worship leader hopes the musicians can play). And he ordered the people, "Advance!"

You can't break down barriers in your life by standing still. You must advance—take ground—move! It takes gutsy people to praise God in the face of opposition. It takes gutsy men and women of God to walk away from the things that once bound them. It takes gutsy people to advance—to move forward.

Joshua did all that God had spoken to him to do. And the presence of the Lord went with them. They marched around the city once and returned to the camp. They did this for six days. They were assessing and praying and getting ready for the meltdown! Then on the seventh day they got up at daybreak and marched around the city in the same manner, except on that day they circled the city seven times.

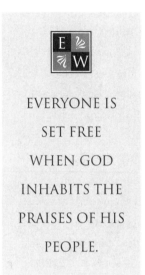

EVERYONE IS SET FREE WHEN GOD INHABITS THE PRAISES OF HIS PEOPLE.

The seventh time around, when the priest sounded the trumpet blast, Joshua commanded the people, "Shout! For the Lord has given you the city! The city and all that is in it is to be devoted to the Lord." Then (v. 20) when the trumpets sounded, the people gave a great shout and the wall collapsed, so every man charged straight in and they took the city, claimed the Promised Land, and devoted it to God!

So it is with you. The presence of God goes with you as you advance into the promises God has given you. It is powerful when you praise God and feel a righteous anger bubble up within you toward your wall. Sometimes crossing your fingers and saying "Please" is not enough to get you loosed and into your Promised Land. Sometimes you need to hold on to God and give a victory shout. A tenacious, explosive shout of praise is a punch in the face of the devil, and it is a declaration of thanksgiving to our awesome God, who keeps His promises to us.

So shout in His presence, and then just stand back and watch the walls collapse. Praise down the big walls in your life. During praise and worship, the prayers—the incense of the saints—are rich and fulfilling. Someone might have come into the service from the middle of evil and darkness, but when surrounded by tenacious, explosive praise, they will see beauty and grace and life abound. Everyone is set free when God inhabits the praises of His people.

You prepare a table before me in the presence of my enemies. You anoint my head with oil; my cup overflows. Surely goodness and love will follow me all the days of my life, and I will dwell in the house of the Lord forever. (Psalm 23:5–6)

Jesus said, "If you hold to my teaching, you are really my disciples. Then you will know the truth, and the truth will set you free" (John 8:31–32).

There are friendships and possibilities of intimate, godly relationships that are kept apart by walls of insecurity. There are great marriages that are locked behind walls of unforgiveness, walls of pride, and walls of mistrust. There are awesome ministries locked behind walls of rebellion and ungodliness. There are healings locked behind walls of fear. And there are the most glorious days of praise ahead of us as we learn to shake off our concern of what people will think and walk in the victory that is reserved for the people who praise God.

Many years ago, when Mark and I first came to Sydney, we met a great couple who were our first close friends at our new church home at Hillsong. Because of my own insecurities, my friendship with Liz went to a certain level, and then I put up a *huge* wall and totally "iced" her out of my life. That "wall" had been built through years of wrong thinking, and I didn't give it over to the lordship of Christ for a long time.

I wanted to proceed with that friendship, and I couldn't. So I retreated into a little shell. I stopped talking to Liz, and I stopped calling her. I desperately wanted to be free to enjoy her friendship, but the wall of insecurity was a biggie! It was real, and I couldn't push past it until I got in the presence of the Lord, yielded my life again, and asked God for help.

I prayed, *God, strip away this wall of insecurity that doesn't want to be hurt by a friendship. I desperately want to give love, but this wall keeps me from receiving it.* Once the wall was broken, it took a few years for us to recover what we had. Now she is one of the dearest people in my life. But I truly regret that lost time.

Walls *are* a waste of time. I get angry because the Enemy comes to steal, to kill, and to rip us off. And yet the Word of God comes to release us. God's presence in our lives brings power to break through, to be liberated, and frees us to enjoy who He is. Praise God, who gives us big hearts and healthy emotions to receive His promises and to love a hurting generation without any walls holding us back.

Chapter Three

ENERGETIC
COMMITMENT

ENERGETIC COMMITMENT

Teach me, O Lord, to follow your decrees; then I will keep them to the
end. Give me understanding, and I will keep your law and obey it with
all my heart. Direct me in the path of your commands, for there
I find delight (Psalm 119:33–35).

Obedience is a word in the Bible many Christians would like to ignore, but Abraham was committed to obeying God. Abraham was filled with inspired zeal to do anything and everything God asked him to do, even when God asked him to offer his beloved son as a sacrifice. Abraham's readiness was evident because after he had heard from God, he rose early the very *next* morning to begin his pilgrimage of obedience.

Perhaps Abraham was eager to obey because he knew he could trust God. Isaac knew they were climbing a mountain to make a sacrifice; they had wood for the altar, and the firepot, but no animal for the sacrifice. He asked his father about it, and we see Abraham's confidence in God's character as he reassured Isaac that the Lord would supply a sacrifice.

When they came to the place that God had told him, Abraham built the altar and laid his son upon it to *offer* Isaac as the sacrifice, just as the Lord had asked him to do. But God stopped Abraham. " 'Do not lay a hand on the boy,' he said. 'Do not do anything to him. Now I know that you fear God, because you have not withheld from me your son, your only son' " (Genesis 22:12). Then Abraham saw a ram caught in a thicket by his horns, and he sacrificed it to the Lord.

The angel of the Lord called to Abraham from heaven a second time
and said, "I swear by myself, declares the Lord, that because you have

done this and have not withheld your son, your only son, I will surely
bless you and make your descendants as numerous as the stars in the
sky and as the sand on the seashore. Your descendants will take
possession of the cities of their enemies, and through your offspring all
nations on earth will be blessed, because you have obeyed me"
(Genesis 22:15–18).

Because Abraham was obedient, God opened up His storehouse of blessing upon His servant. Isn't it awesome that God is willing to bless all the nations of the earth because of one man's obedience? What might God do with our obedience?

SUBMISSION ONLY HAPPENS WHEN WE OBEY *EVEN THOUGH WE DON'T AGREE* WITH WHAT WE HAVE BEEN ASKED TO DO.

Obedience means submission (another word we all love); submission is habitual yielding to authority. The word *yielding* even sounds awful! To yield requires commitment. We are to decide to obey, and then commit and submit. It is easy to enthusiastically submit to authority when everything is lovely, but submission is not submission until we don't agree. Submission only happens when we obey *even though we don't agree* with what we have been asked to do. Until we obey even when we disagree, we have never submitted at all! We were in agreement, but we weren't in submission.

Why are people so afraid to obey—to commit, to submit, and to habitually yield to authority? I believe obedience requires a response of trust and a commitment to that response. Obedience requires an actual follow-through, and people are not great at finishing what they begin. People generally are all great starters, because everyone likes quick, instantaneous provision and change.

But most people moan if they have to wait thirty seconds longer than normal at the drive-thru! Everyone wants immediate results; few people are prepared to wait. But God is a builder, not a magician. He is a builder of life, and the finest buildings always take time.

Life's journey will always include a few valleys. But if you don't give up trusting God, you will enjoy great victory on the other side of the valley. God has plans for you that are *way* beyond anything you could ever ask or think. God promises to work all things together for our good, but often we are not willing to endure and obey Him while we wait for results. We are willing to respond, but often we're not willing to put the commitment into that response that would allow us to enjoy the final victory.

We fail when we try to obey God in our own power. We were never called to live this supernatural life by natural means. We were created to a godly life through the infilling power of the Holy Spirit. God's Word says, " 'Not by might nor by power, but by my Spirit,' says the Lord Almighty" (Zechariah 4:6). When we receive Jesus as Lord and Savior, we receive His Holy Spirit to dwell in us and give us the power to be witnesses of His glory. Salvation rewires us to live a life of purpose through the power of the Holy Spirit. That's why we should adapt Paul's prayer from Ephesians 3:16–19, saying,

> GOD HAS PLANS FOR YOU THAT ARE *WAY* BEYOND ANYTHING YOU COULD EVER ASK OR THINK.

Lord, I pray that out of your glorious riches you will strengthen me with power through the Spirit in my inner being, so that Christ may dwell in my heart through faith. And I pray that I, being rooted and established in love, may have power, together with all the saints, to grasp how wide and long and high and deep is the love of

Christ, and to know this love that surpasses knowledge—that I may be filled to the measure of all the fullness of God. I know that you are able to do immeasurably more than all I could ask or imagine, according to your power that is at work within me. To you be glory in the church and in Christ Jesus throughout all generations, for ever and ever! Amen.

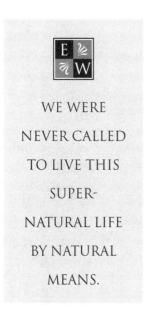

WE WERE
NEVER CALLED
TO LIVE THIS
SUPER-
NATURAL LIFE
BY NATURAL
MEANS.

Before I was saved, I thought obedience meant adherence to laws and rules. Obedience was a response of duty and was purely a cerebral decision. I did not consider obedience a heartfelt decision: it was fact-based. In the Old Testament, people obeyed because it meant death if they didn't, so obedience was a fairly good option! But in this new life in Christ, under a new covenant, obedience is an issue of the heart. Obeying God is not a fact-based decision; it is a faith-based decision.

We can obey the Lord because He requires it, regardless of what we can see. But it is best to obey because we trust God. Trust does not observe obedience through the eyes of man but by seeing God's instruction through the eyes of the Spirit. If we trust God's character, as Abraham did, we can trust that our obedience will never take us to a place that we don't want to be.

Charles Swindoll once said, "The best proof of your love for the Lord is obedience. Nothing more, nothing less, nothing else." That's fantastic! Obedience is not for the fainthearted; obedience is for the warrior. Obedience is for the one who can stand strong despite circumstances and say "Yes!" to God and no to themselves. That is obedience. Obedience requires strength and stamina.

We are the army of the Lord, and we can only go so far if we do not have complete obedience and complete commitment. Obedience to God is not a mental discipline; it is a yielded heart to God. Obedience is a beautiful part of worship. I love standing in the middle of people who are consumed with God, consumed with honoring Him in their praise and worship through song.

There are always people who make a choice not to enter in to the corporate act of worship. In the middle of the incredible presence of God, they stop short of entering in because they lack obedience to His invitation to come into His presence. They fold their arms, lock up on the inside, and basically say, "I will not worship God."

I am desperate to be someone who obeys the Lord. I keep my heartbeat in tune with His heartbeat. I want to be in sync with Him. I want to inspire others to obey Him, so that they can fulfill all that they were born to enjoy. If we don't obey, we disobey. There is no middle ground, and God detests the middle ground. He doesn't like lukewarm. So don't let fear of obedience rule and bind you. Fear will cause you to stay still while everyone else moves forward. Fear will leave you in the middle of nowhere. Commit to obey God with enthusiasm and get up early to do what He calls you to do.

THE FEAR OF THE LORD IS A DEEP, REVERENTIAL SENSE OF OUR ACCOUNT-ABILITY TO HIM.

FEAR THE LORD

The fear of the Lord inspires obedience. This reverent fear of God is different from the fear that binds. God said, "Oh, that their hearts would be inclined to fear me and keep all my commands always, so that it might go well with them and their children forever!" (Deuteronomy 5:29).

forever is a great promise! Yet if we do not obey, if we start looking at our lives with human eyes and not eyes of the spirit, we hinder that promise from God. He wants our hearts to fear Him. He wants us to keep His commands always so that it might go well with us and with our children—forever.

The fear of the Lord is a deep, reverential sense of our accountability to Him. He is our Comforter, and we can talk to Him as our best friend. But He is also the Creator of the universe, the Alpha and Omega, the beginning and the end, the first and the last. He is our salvation, He is our healer, He is our provider, He is our perfect Lamb of God.

The Lord listens to our praise and worship. He listens to what we say about Him to others. Malachi 3:16 says,

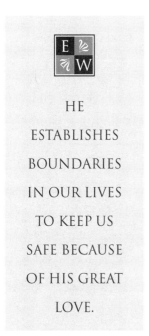

HE ESTABLISHES BOUNDARIES IN OUR LIVES TO KEEP US SAFE BECAUSE OF HIS GREAT LOVE.

Then those who feared the Lord talked with each other, and the Lord listened and heard. A scroll of remembrance was written in his presence concerning those who feared the Lord and honored his name. "They will be mine," says the Lord Almighty, "in the day when I make up my treasured possession. I will spare them, just as in compassion a man spares his son who serves him. And you will again see the distinction between the righteous and the wicked, between those who serve God and those who do not.

As Christians, we are children of the living God with incredible access into His throne room. But because He is a loving Father, He requires our obedience. If parents left their children outside alone without guidelines and even said, "Play on the freeway. Whatever you want to do is fine. . . ." we would all agree that they were not great parents.

The Lord loves us and gives us guidelines that will cause events to go well with us and with our children forever. He establishes boundaries in our lives to keep us safe because of His great love. He is committed to helping us become all He created us to be. If He did not require obedience, imagine what a mess we would be in!

I love the Holy Spirit because He faithfully guides us. It's still our choice to obey, but if we don't yield to God's authority, we will end up going in circles around the mountain instead of onward to greater adventures. May we all fear the Lord and reverence Him. May we all receive the blessings that obedience brings into our lives.

PUT YOUR FAITH IN GOD

Trust in the Lord with all your heart and lean not on
your own understanding. (Proverbs 3:5)

I've learned to always trust in God and not to be led by what I see. To obey God's Word rather than popular opinion and to trust His perfect timing is always a character-building lesson! I challenge you to pick up the banner that says "Whatever It Takes" and put it over your life in complete obedience. Surrender to the incredible heart of our Lord, because His ways are higher than our ways. Sometimes it's hard to understand, but it is a reality that His ways are better than ours every single time.

When Mother Teresa was young, she told her mother that she wanted to go into the ministry. Her mother had other plans for her sweet Teresa, but she obeyed the Lord and told her daughter, "Put your hand in God's hand and walk all the way with Him—all the way with Him to completion." And the world watched Teresa do that with the glory of God as a banner over her. Her banner could have read, "Whatever It Takes."

At the beginning of the second millennium, Saint Francis of Assisi wrote the following prayer:

WHATEVER IT TAKES

LORD, MAKE ME AN INSTRUMENT OF YOUR PEACE.
WHERE THERE IS HATRED LET ME SOW LOVE
WHERE THERE IS INJURY, PARDON
WHERE THERE IS DISCORD, UNITY
WHERE THERE IS DOUBT, FAITH
WHERE THERE IS ERROR, TRUTH
WHERE THERE IS DESPAIR, HOPE
WHERE THERE IS DARKNESS, LIGHT
AND WHERE THERE IS SADNESS, JOY.
DIVINE MASTER, GRANT ME THAT I MAY SEEK
NOT SO MUCH TO BE CONSOLED BUT TO CONSOLE
NOT SO MUCH TO BE UNDERSTOOD AS TO UNDERSTAND
NOT SO MUCH TO BE LOVED AS TO LOVE
FOR IT IS IN GIVING THAT WE RECEIVE
IT IS IN LOSING OURSELVES THAT WE FIND OURSELVES
IT IS IN PARDONING THAT WE ARE PARDONED
AND IT IS IN DYING THAT WE ARE BORN TO ETERNAL LIFE.

—PRAYER OF SAINT FRANCIS

COUNT THE COST

We treasure something that has cost us personally. If we've worked really hard for something and it is finally ours, we hold it carefully.

Children who are constantly given everything they ask for without responsibility to the price have no regard for the value of their possessions. The goals in our lives will cost, but we should be willing to count that cost. Whatever the price to gain Christ and His love is worth it.

"Shout to the Lord" is a song that is popular all over the world. People have actually said to me that they wished they had written it. But for me, it was a very expensive song to write. The words to that song came out of a personal and difficult time in my life that cost me dearly. If I had not landed on the right side of a breakthrough, that time in my life would have been too expensive. But now I wouldn't trade any of the hardships I faced then, for I can see that they gave me strength to break through restrictive walls and finish on the right side of becoming an overcomer.

But if I had stopped just before the wall came down, it would have been far too expensive a cost on my life. My inner man couldn't afford the price of the pain I bore at that time, but something rose up within me—

I WOULD SAY THAT THE MAJORITY OF PEOPLE DON'T PAY THAT PRICE OF OBEDIENCE THAT WOULD LEAD THEM THROUGH THE WALL THAT HIDES THEIR PROMISED LAND.

Something that wasn't me. The Spirit of God made me push on and through to the other side of the wall that kept me from God's great promises for my life. But to get through to those promises required a great investment of my life.

Sometime you may need to count the cost and push through to God's Promised Land; most likely it will be on the other side of a wall of hardship. I would say that the majority of people don't pay that price of obedience that would lead them through the wall that hides their Promised Land. They retreat, and they never find out what was just on the other side.

"Wisdom is supreme; therefore get wisdom. *Though it cost all you have,* get understanding" (Proverbs 4:7, emphasis added).

Revelation 21:6–7 says, "It is done. I am the Alpha and the Omega, the Beginning and the End. To him who is thirsty I will give to drink *without cost* from the spring of the water of life. *He who overcomes will inherit all this,* and I will be his God and he will be my son" (emphasis added). It interested me to learn that the spring of the water of life is free, and he who overcomes will inherit all this. People read the first half of the verse and say, "Excellent, living water to quench my spiritual thirst is free!" But the next line explains that there is a cost involved in order to have access to the inheritance.

One must be an overcomer in order to inherit the promises of God. An overcomer is one who will resist any competition and any schemes of the Enemy. God says that the one who is an overcomer (prepared to do whatever it takes) will inherit all this—free access to the springs of the water of life.

Valuable things cost something. We must decide whether we are willing to pay the price. I want to be a valuable leader in the house of God; therefore I must be prepared to count the cost needed to become that person. Being a great parent costs us time. Being a great singer or musician requires discipline, practice, and more practice. Being a great spouse takes love and lots of it!

How valuable something is to you determines the price you are willing to pay for it. Every time you pay the price it makes you stand taller. It makes you stand stronger, and you become a bigger person in Christ. If you are facing a cost, don't pull back from it. Pay the price to be an overcomer. Be accountable to someone if you need help to endure; talk to your friends, pastors, mentors, your accountability group, or your cell group. Godly counsel will encourage and inspire you to pay the asking price.

Be enthusiastically committed to pay whatever it takes to receive the prize. When I look at the high price tags that have come with some of life's lessons, I'm so very glad that I chose to pay. Increase your commitment to God's way to His Promised Land for you. The level of commitment that was of great price for you last year is not so radical anymore. There is always a new level to reach in your relationship with God, with a new price tag of obedience to pay. It's worth the price—it cost Jesus everything to offer it to you. Be committed to obey God with enthusiasm, not because you are trying to impress people around you, but because of your love for Jesus. Do whatever it takes to see His kingdom advance.

Count the cost and do it beautifully and do it with joy. Once you commit to that decision, you won't even consider it anymore. Commitment establishes a "done deal" in your mind.

The Father is looking for people who will not be swayed to give up the race. He is looking for people who will march around their Jericho one more day, one more time, even as many times as it takes to see the wall come down that is keeping them away from His promises. He is looking for people who have counted the cost and have chosen to follow Him.

I gave up my rights a long time ago. This life is just not mine to live. That's a done deal. I encourage you to make that decision too. Pay the price and just do it. You will never wonder if God is true to His promises once you learn to quickly obey Him with committed enthusiasm.

Hold on to the certainty of this promise from God:

When God made his promise to Abraham, since there was no one
greater for him to swear by, he swore by himself, saying, "I will surely
bless you and give you many descendants." And so after
waiting patiently, Abraham received what was promised.
Men swear by someone greater than themselves, and the oath confirms
what is said and puts an end to all argument. Because God wanted to
make the unchanging nature of his purpose very clear to the heirs of
what was promised, he confirmed it with an oath. God did this so that,
by two unchangeable things in which it is impossible for God to lie, we
who have fled to take hold of the hope offered to us may be greatly
encouraged. We have this hope as an anchor for the soul,
firm and secure. (Hebrews 6:13–19)

When God makes a promise, it is settled. Perseverance is the way in
which you receive that covenant of promise in your life. Dare to commit
your life totally to God. Dare to persevere, and see what that perseverance will bring forth. Hang in there, because the promise of God is
unchanging; it is certain. It's your choice to receive the promise. Make a
commitment to enthusiastically serve Him whatever the cost.

HAVE YOUR WAY

THIS YEARNING DEEP WITHIN ME
REACHES OUT TO YOU
YOUR OIL OF JOY FOR MOURNING
SOAKS ME, MAKES ME NEW
AND I WILL GO
TO YOUR SECRET PLACE
BOW MY KNEE
TO YOUR GLORIOUS THRONE
HAVE YOUR WAY
IN MY HEART, O LORD
HAVE YOUR WAY
I NEED YOU, HOLY SPIRIT
FIRE TO MY SOUL
CONSUME MY TOTAL BEING
JESUS, TAKE CONTROL

1998 DARLENE ZSCHECH
HILLSONG PUBLISHING

Chapter Four

EMOTIONAL
FERVOR

EMOTIONAL FERVOR

Creative people are driven by a passion to express their inner dreams. If you are blessed with a creative gift, then you know how the emotional or "feeling" side of our personalities actually makes us great at what we do. But our greatest emotional strengths also have the potential to be our "undoing." Have you ever become angry or confused after a time of creative expression because you were disappointed with the outcome of your work? Have you ever agreed with enthusiasm to sing a song or play an instrument for a special event only to spin into depression afterward because you felt you were not so great?

Perhaps you have had an opportunity to see a dream come true but then found its reality fell short of your expectations. Perhaps you hear a song in your head, but you can't write it down. Maybe you set a goal, and when it wasn't achieved by the time you wanted it, you gave it up, and now it's causing that emotional well in you to be filled with negativity. I believe you may have felt some or even all of these emotions at some time in your life, for I have been tossed about by such emotions many, many times. For too long, rather than ruling my emotions, I let those negative emotions rule.

So many times I have sat in that depressing place; it might have lasted an hour; it might have lasted a day, a week, or even an entire month. For some of you, emotional depression may have clung to you for years. Even a few minutes is a long time for oppressive thinking to hold you back. Every time depression tempts my emotions, I think to myself later, *Entertaining these thoughts is so dumb; I do not want to be this person. Negativity and depression are a waste of time and a waste of energy as a creative person. I know this is not the divine plan of God for me to live like this.*

HAVE YOU EVER AGREED WITH ENTHUSIASM TO SING A SONG OR PLAY AN INSTRUMENT FOR A SPECIAL EVENT ONLY TO SPIN INTO DEPRESSION AFTERWARD BECAUSE YOU FELT YOU WERE NOT SO GREAT?

Musicians, writers, painters, and dancers are among the creative people who are often labeled as moody, focused, intense, passionate, emotional, fragile, weird, and just too "in touch with their feelings." Art galleries often post biographical captions by artists' names describing them as "tortured artists." Too often creative people live in turmoil and torment because their emotional side is the part of themselves that can bring such depth of expression. But emotions can also keep them from great achievements.

Psalm 88 expresses a creative person's "down" side:

O Lord, the God who saves me, day and night I cry out before you. May my prayer come before you; turn your ear to my cry. For my soul is full of trouble and my life draws near the grave.
I am counted among those who go down to the pit; I am like a man without strength. I am set apart with the dead, like the slain who lie in the grave, whom you remember no more, who are cut off from your care.
You have put me in the lowest pit, in the darkest depths. Your wrath lies heavily upon me; you have overwhelmed me with all your waves. Selah
You have taken from me my closest friends and have made me repulsive to them. I am confined and cannot escape; my eyes are dim with grief.
I call to you, O Lord, every day; I spread out my hands to you. Do you

*show your wonders to the dead? Do those who are dead
rise up and praise you? Selah
Is your love declared in the grave, your faithfulness in destruction? Are
your wonders known in the place of darkness, or your
righteous deeds in the land of oblivion?
But I cry to you for help, O Lord; in the morning my prayer comes before
you. Why, O Lord, do you reject me and hide your face from me? From
my youth I have been afflicted and close to death; I have
suffered your terrors and am in despair.
Your wrath has swept over me; your terrors have destroyed me. All day
long they surround me like a flood; they have completely engulfed me.
You have taken my companions and loved ones from me;
the darkness is my closest friend.*

Ever had days like that? When dreariness and despair go on and on?

Personally, I love Psalm 89:1, which says, "I will sing of the Lord's great love forever." Obviously, our creative songwriter was feeling much better when he wrote the latter psalm!

When a creative person with an artistic temperament is not yielded to the Holy Spirit and the lordship of Christ, Psalm 88 is an accurate picture of how he or she may view life. Creative people can tend to get isolated and then wallow in self-pity. But "God sets the lonely in families" (Psalm 68:6) because He said it isn't good for us to be alone. When we yield our lives over to Him, He puts us with each other so that we can encourage one

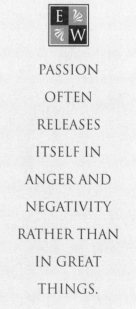

PASSION
OFTEN
RELEASES
ITSELF IN
ANGER AND
NEGATIVITY
RATHER THAN
IN GREAT
THINGS.

another, so that we can sing of the Lord's greatness and love together.

Having time to be alone is a valid need for most creative people. Over 90 percent of the creative people I know like solitude. They enjoy that time when they can be alone to think and create, to write, play, dream, imagine, and express themselves artistically. But when the desire to be alone becomes selfish, it becomes a very destructive thing. Solitude is great if it is yielded to the patterns of the Lord, who withdrew to a solitary place before ministering to the masses. Solitude should not be used to withdraw one's gifts from humanity but to refill oneself for ministry to others by yielding to Jesus Christ.

When Michelangelo was twenty-two years old, he wrote to his father and said, "Do not wonder if I have sometimes written irritable letters, for I often suffer great distresses of mind and temper." Even as a young man he was full of depth and brilliance, but he was basically saying, "Don't worry about me, Dad. These emotions are within me, and I just don't quite know what to do with them."

Passion often releases itself in anger and negativity rather than in great things. Van Gogh was manic-depressive and driven to suicide at thirty-seven. Too much solitude rendered him unable to cope with life anymore. Tragically, the other side of the scale to the great works of a creative person is great despair. I think that is why creative people are often misunderstood. But emotions can be managed and directed toward Christ's purpose rather than directing them internally and never yielding them over to the redemptive power of Jesus.

We are all designed to be creative, in the image of our creative Lord. Even as creative, healthy, Word-loving Christians, we still experience a vast range of emotions. The goal is not to let our "feelings" rule us but to submit our emotions to the Lord. As we yield our negative thoughts to Him, He gives us His positive Word. We can truly say, "The joy of the Lord is my strength" (Nehemiah 8:10).

I'm not easily depressed; I am normally an enthusiastic person. Even before I was saved, I was a joyful person. But because I'm creative, I never knew what to do with the melancholy emotions that sometimes overcame me. I could always write songs and lyrics, but every time I spent too much time alone, my work would get very, very dark. I just never knew what to do about it.

When I accepted Christ, He put a fresh and exciting perspective on my view of the world. Jesus brought life and enthusiasm to my creative moments. The music I wrote before giving my life to the Lord had not been able to fulfill in me a sense of purpose. The success I had achieved hadn't satisfied my sense of destiny. The money I had earned hadn't given me a sense of fulfillment. None of those rewards put life-giving joy into our perspective of the world. It is only when we use our gifts to lift the name of Christ that we truly satisfy those creative impulses in us. When I saw the world from Jesus' perspective, I was able to break through my inward emotions and feel His passion for others.

I actually had to step out of singing for a little while when I was first saved because I wasn't quite sure how my creative gifts could be used for Him. My internal emotional structure was trying to work it all out. How could I now sing under the lordship of Christ, when I had always been allowed to wallow in me, myself, and I? But when I finally learned to work creatively under the lordship of Christ, I could hear Him call me back to His way. When despair would raise up its destructive suggestions, He would say in my heart, "No. Don't go there. Those emotions, those negative ones, will bow down to my lordship."

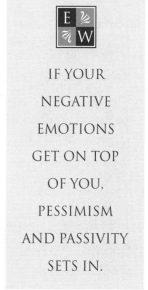

IF YOUR NEGATIVE EMOTIONS GET ON TOP OF YOU, PESSIMISM AND PASSIVITY SETS IN.

If your negative emotions get on top of you, pessimism and passivity sets in. To fight those dark times in your life, ask the Lord to reign over your creative drive. Ask the Lord to rule over your desire for attention. Creative people often feel this is a need that must be fulfilled. I wasn't negative, but I felt the need for attention.

Sometimes if attention is not gained by their gifts, creative people will try to gain assurance by telling everyone how "untalented" they are—desperately hoping and expecting that someone will contradict them! This is false humility, and it is a form of pride that says, "Love me because I am gifted!" Whereas true humility says, "Let me use my gift to show you how loved you are in Christ."

ONE OF THE WORST EFFECTS OF LETTING OUR NEGATIVE EMOTIONS GET ON TOP OF US IS THAT THEY MAKE US FEEL ALIENATED FROM GOD.

Often people become cynical when their negative emotions rule them. Eventually they start seeing the bad side of *everything*. One day I was reading through the feedback forms from a Hillsong conference. I really wanted to know what people thought was good, what lectures were helpful and which ones weren't. We work hard to make sure our conferences are of a high standard, so I definitely want to know if there are things we can improve. Ninety-nine forms out of a hundred were positive, so when I found a negative review I took careful notice.

One man at the conference must have had the worst day of his entire life! On a scale of one to ten, where ten is the goal and one is shocking, this guy had written "one" right throughout the form—about everything! He even criticized all the preachers that we had invited from overseas, and suggested they all jump back on a plane and go home! After reading in disbelief, I started to feel compassion for this guy. By the time I finished reading his review, I honestly wanted to sit down with him and ask, "How are you doing? What's happening in your world?" Not because he was critical of what we had done—I sincerely want to improve!

But he didn't base any criticisms specifically on what we had done badly; everything he wrote was based on his own emotional chaos, which clouded his whole world. This was someone in the creative faculty, and it was so obvious that he was a frustrated artist who just did not know what else to do. Rather than deal with his emotional state, he thought he'd take out his dissatisfaction on everything around him to make himself feel better. What a terrible way to live!

One of the worst effects of letting our negative emotions get on top of us is that they make us feel alienated from God. If things are going well, we tend to feel that God likes us. But if things are going badly, we often feel that God is angry with us. We mustn't depend on feelings. Our creative thoughts need to be filled with the truth of God's Word to keep us built up, edified, and productive.

Proverbs 25:28 says, "Like a city whose walls are broken down is a man who lacks self-control." If we lack self-control over our emotional state, we are like an unprotected city that is vulnerable to attacks and subject to chaos. God wants us to be creative people who walk with strength and security.

My husband, Mark, loves to buy old books. He found one for me called *Master Musicians: Stories of Romantic Lives*. It's amazing to read the stories of Bach, Schubert, Mozart, and Beethoven. There were a couple of exceptions, but many of these awesome musicians had chaotic emotional lives. They drove themselves nuts—and everybody else around them as well!

As I read this beautiful book, I thought, *Lord Jesus, we are living in a new day where we worshipers need to be strong. We need to stand out in front to be the herald of God in the earth. We need to do what we are called to do. We need to proclaim the Good News of the gospel, to worship and praise you. We can't just become "stories of romantic lives." We have to be living and breathing testimonies of the greatness of God.* That's really what we are to aim for. When we surrender the emotional part of our lives to the Lord, we will be able to stand strong for Him.

I have the privilege of leadership over the musicians and singers at Hillsong Church, but if I don't zip up the emotional part of me, sometimes I won't lead others effectively. I have found that the soft side of being a musician and the strong side of being a leader sometimes work in opposition to each other. On the one hand I want to be caressing, and on the other I have to be correcting! I want to be compassionate and lovely all the time, but a leader must be strong enough to pick people up and take them on to their destined place in life. It isn't appropriate for a leader to talk about how disaster-filled his or her life is. Leaders must get their eyes off themselves to inspire others to get up and walk on with the Lord. I have learned some practical keys to controlling my emotions that would be helpful to everyone wanting to gain control of their emotions.

DETERMINE TO BE JOYFUL AND GLAD REGARDLESS OF THE CIRCUMSTANCES AROUND YOU.

Dwell on Truth

The first key to controlling negative emotions is to pray that God will give you ears that are sensitive to God's truth. Often the creative heart is attracted to reports of "gloom and doom." If no one says to them, "Okay, let's focus on God's report," they will get stuck in pessimism and despair. If you have the tendencies of a melancholy heart, pray David's psalm, saying, "Make me to hear joy and gladness and be satisfied" (Psalm 51:8 AMP). This prayer will change you because God answers prayer that is in accordance with His Word.

Determine to be joyful and glad regardless of the circumstances around you. Discipline your mind to dwell on the truth. A psalm that has helped me to develop healthy self-esteem and maintain emotional self-control is Psalm 139:5–6, 3–16, 23–24:

You hem me in—behind and before; you have laid your hand upon me.
Such knowledge is too wonderful for me, too lofty for me to attain.
For you created my inmost being; you knit me together in my mother's
womb. I praise you because I am fearfully and wonderfully made;
your works are wonderful, I know that full well.
My frame was not hidden from you when I was made in the secret
place. When I was woven together in the depths of the earth, your eyes
saw my unformed body. All the days ordained for me were
written in your book before one of them came to be.
Search me, O God, and know my heart; test me and know my anxious
thoughts. See if there is any offensive way in me, and
lead me in the way everlasting.

When I feel tempted to lose control of my emotions, I pray, *Lord, lead me because you know I tend to run toward what is gloomy. Teach me how to run toward what is great. Teach me how to be a strong person. Teach me, God, how to yield my emotions to you and to dwell on your truth.*

Develop Your Unseen Life of Worship

C. S. Lewis describes worship as "inner health made audible." Worshiping God establishes our inner health, or emotional state, in the light of who God is. Too often we set our emotions in the light of who other people are. We can become discouraged if we compare ourselves to others. Rather than looking at others, we should look at God by worshiping Him. Spending time alone with Him will give us knowledge of His great love for us and help us to view ourselves as God sees us. Worship restores our inner health.

Worship is the most selfless experience that your nature is capable of because it takes your eyes off of your weakness and on to God's power. Worship God when you feel weak. Worship God when you feel vulnerable. When in your time of solitude your creativity hits a dark moment, worship God. When you feel tempted, worship God. When you are angry, worship God. When you are disappointed, worship God. Worship

God when your emotions become unstable, and watch how quickly your inner health is restored.

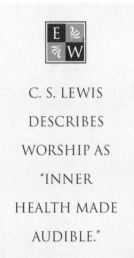

C. S. LEWIS DESCRIBES WORSHIP AS "INNER HEALTH MADE AUDIBLE."

Have a Sense of Humor

Those *Funniest Home Videos* shows on TV make us laugh when we watch someone do something like fall off a stage while trying to seriously perform or sing. It's easy to recognize that they need a sense of humor to get through such an embarrassing moment. We've all done something embarrassing, yet we quickly forget to look at the humor in it when we're the one on center stage. Most of our failures are not nearly as dramatic as the ones we see on TV, but we creative people tend to torture ourselves for weeks over the tiniest mishap.

Sometimes we just need to get a sense of humor, because everyone makes mistakes. The greatest people make mistakes, and they're great because they learn from them. If at all possible, it's nice to make mistakes when we're alone, but it usually doesn't work that way! Unfortunately, most of our mistakes will be *very* public!

Stop punishing yourself for your mistakes. You will remember them far longer than anyone else will. Taking yourself too seriously will destroy your creativity and your joy. Have a good laugh at yourself. Ecclesiastes 7:16 says, "Do not be overrighteous, neither be overwise—why destroy yourself?" Basically the Word is saying, "Don't go too far that way, and don't go too far the other way, because it'll blow you up." Proverbs 17:22 says, "A cheerful heart is good medicine, but a crushed spirit dries up the bones."

We all need to have a good sense of humor. I'll never forget the time we were recording a video album, and we were actually in the middle of a worship service. I was singing, but I could see the stage manager waving at me and telling me to stop. I thought, *Stop? We're in the middle of worship here!*

But she kept waving at me and said, "Mark says to stop!" I thought, *If Mark says to stop, I'm stopping. After all, he is my husband!*

So I asked, "What's the problem?" I was expecting some sort of technical failure, and we would need to restart the song. By now the congregation was waiting and wondering what was going on.

I couldn't believe the stage manager's answer: "We have to fix your hair." I was totally embarrassed! To lighten the situation, we asked the whole church to take a break and fix their hair. Everyone had a laugh, and I was grateful that the church had a good sense of humor.

Surround Yourself With the Right People

Try to put yourself in an environment where you are able to laugh and be lifted by others. Surround yourself with people who won't tolerate your moody melancholy days but will pick you up and help you to see the bright side of life. That's why Jesus was so good to give us the church family. Can you imagine being newly saved and being all by yourself?

We need the church; we need the balance of the family, the team. We need each other. We need to be thrown into this environment that makes us strong believers. The environment of faith makes us who we are in Christ and allows us to grow. We need to be in an environment where we hear the Word and where it can grow in us so that we become strong and no longer ruled by our emotions.

TRY TO PUT YOURSELF IN AN ENVIRONMENT WHERE YOU ARE ABLE TO LAUGH AND BE LIFTED BY OTHERS.

When I was still singing professionally in the secular arena, I often went into situations where there were brilliant, creative people, but they weren't Christians. The first hour everyone would be working hard and doing well emotionally. But after a few hours the working relationships consistently became tense because the people didn't have the depth of God's "3-D" perspective on their life and work. They only had the two-dimensional perspective, and if their performance didn't measure up to their expectations, they came crashing down on themselves and on everyone around them. I am not concerned about their public behavior, but I am concerned about what happens to artists who are alone with those self-condemning thoughts and who have no Savior to redeem their world.

It is important to position yourself near great people who can help you, challenge you, and spur you on. I love Pastor Brian Houston's honest style of leadership at Hillsong Church. If we make a mistake, Pastor Brian doesn't say, "Oh, friend, I understand that you tried, I know you've spent time on this, so let's pray about it."

No, Pastor Brian is more likely to say, "What was that? That was awful! Don't do that again!" The truth is out in the open and it has nothing to do with personal issues or agendas. It's clear he thinks you are the same awesome person, but he plainly states, "Let's definitely do things a different way next time." A temperamental person may find his style of leadership difficult to be around at first because it's quite "in-your-face," but for the long term, his straightforwardness is awesome. It's a fantastic style of leadership for brave, creative people.

If you don't want to be challenged, and you don't mind living below the line of excellence, then don't seek strong leaders. But I am grateful for strong leadership, because I know what I am like without it—and it's not good. I know that being matched with my husband, who is a strong man, has been the best thing for me. And being surrounded by strong leaders and friends who can laugh with me has been my saving grace.

Learn How to Deal With Disappointment

You may feel overlooked by church leadership, or if you are a musician you may feel unfulfilled musically, but the problem is not with the church. God has given each of us the keys to solve our own issues of discontent. I have learned that if I have the right attitude, all of my musical ambitions can be fulfilled within the local church. My sense of fulfillment is not because our worship albums are successful. I learned many years ago that fulfillment is a condition of the heart. Your satisfaction for life must come from your own heart and not from applause, approval, or permission from others.

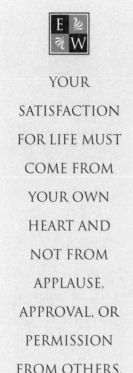

YOUR SATISFACTION FOR LIFE MUST COME FROM YOUR OWN HEART AND NOT FROM APPLAUSE, APPROVAL, OR PERMISSION FROM OTHERS.

Most of those who are without a Savior, who are outside the covenant of Christ, run hard through life without regard to anyone in their way who gets knocked over. Their attitude is "It's all about me!" But in God's economy, everything is just the opposite.

Fulfillment comes from worshiping Him, not from having others worship you. Pleasure comes from using your creative gifts to glorify His name, not your own. Gratification is not from making the "Bestseller of the Week" but by grasping the fact that your creative gift is used for something that matters for eternity. If you understand this, you will learn to swallow hard, maintain a free spirit, and grow in faith, love, patience, and contentment.

Paul said, "I have learned to be content whatever the circumstances" (Philippians 4:11). We all need to learn how to be content where we are and continue to faithfully worship God. Long-term fulfillment is a life that is built on being faithful in and out of season. Commitment to building up others leads to true contentment.

The best place to use our gifts to encourage people is in the local church. This kind of service is a true act of worship. But I've seen people become quite unhappy after a short run of service with the team at church, and they leave full of discontent and disappointment. Their emotions motivate them the wrong way, so they quit. They may be gone for a season, and then they come back and try again. When it gets too hard, they repeat their cycle of escape, and their unfulfilled dreams continue.

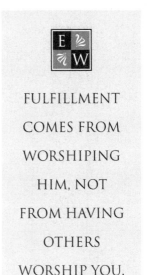

FULFILLMENT COMES FROM WORSHIPING HIM, NOT FROM HAVING OTHERS WORSHIP YOU.

They can't seem to break away from discontentment, feeling misunderstood, and feeling "used" by the church. They may have been praying, "God, use me," but then as soon He does, they complain that they feel used!

Don't wince if God answers your prayer and uses you! Do all that you do as unto Him so that your pleasure is from knowing that He sees your act of service. This will help you deal with the disappointment of feeling overlooked by others. Surrender your desire to be noticed, and give your creative gifts in service to the Lord. Once you let them go and die to the need to be "fulfilled," you will find contentment.

You will end up frustrated or disappointed until you honestly pray, *God, I know that all these years I've said, "Please, use me," but I've actually had my own agenda behind that request. I wanted to be noticed by others. But this time, Lord, I really mean it—whatever it takes to build your kingdom—use me for your glory and not my own.* God's ways are higher than our ways, and His timing is always perfect.

Sometimes we might have to arrest our words and say, "I will not confess this negative opinion anymore. I will not talk like this anymore. I will worship God and dwell on the great things He does. I will let Him work in and through me." We need to learn to keep our hands off of God's plan and walk away from disappointment so that we can be strong and effective in the house of God.

If you don't manage your emotions, you'll be disappointed with yourself and never reach your destiny. If you are driven by your emotions, you will run in circles without ever moving toward your goals. Learn to build your life on something stronger than your own fickle emotions. Accept the challenge to manage your own emotions rather than letting your emotions manage you.

Learn to be content with little, and learn how to be content with much, and you will become stronger emotionally. Don't become as a master musician whose life is featured in a book as a tragic, tortured genius. We have a covenant promise from Jesus that says we don't have to live in that place. Worship the Lord with your contentment.

Sometimes when I have found it hard to lift myself out of the "land of melancholy," and I know the Enemy is jumping on the back of it and trying to steal my dream, I have had to rise up and shout my melancholy down. I

COMMITMENT TO BUILDING UP OTHERS LEADS TO TRUE CONTENTMENT.

have had to shout it down and say, "You will not rule me. I will rule you."

Then that melancholy part of my temperament helps me express the depth of my feelings and pour them into a song of worship. But I've learned not to allow that temperament to rule my emotions. In times when I feel overwhelmed, I shout to the Lord! I bury those melancholy blues in a shout, and declare that it will bow down to the name of Jesus. Learn the power of controlling your emotions, so that your emotional fervor can rise up in spirit and in truth as an extravagant worshiper!

LORD, I GIVE MYSELF

LORD, I GIVE MYSELF
I TRUST IN YOU, MIGHTY GOD
MY SAVIOR
AND YOUR MERCY AND LOVE
OVERFLOWS, AND MY SOUL REJOICES
LORD, SHOW ME YOUR WAYS
GUIDE MY STEPS
LEAD ME TO YOUR RIGHTEOUSNESS
AND THE LIGHT OF YOUR LOVE
TAKES MY FEAR AWAY
'CAUSE I KNOW YOU WALK BEFORE ME
OH, MY SHEPHERD,
YOU LET ME REST IN YOUR ARMS, YOU COMFORT ME
AND EVERYWHERE THAT I GO
I'M NOT ALONE, MIGHTY GOD
I KNOW YOU'RE WITH ME

1994 DARLENE ZSCHECH
HILLSONG PUBLISHING

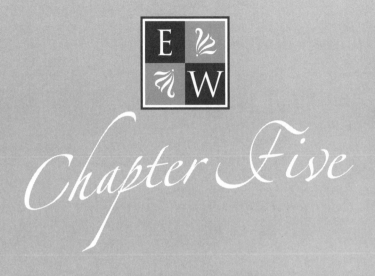

Chapter Five

ELEGANT
DREAMS

ELEGANT DREAMS

The Lord is near to all who call on him, to all who call on him in truth.
He fulfills the desires of those who fear him; he hears their cry
and saves them. (Psalm 145:18–19)

Worshiping God causes our deepest desires to come to pass. Psalm 37:4 says, "Delight yourself in the Lord and he will give you the desires of your heart." As long as we *delight* ourselves in the Lord (the heart of a worshiper), He will be faithful to His promise. In fact, the Word says clearly that "the Lord *longs* to be gracious to you; he rises to show you compassion. For the Lord is a God of justice. Blessed are all who wait for him!" (Isaiah 30:18). God *longs* to show you His grace and compassion!

Desire is such a powerful force in our lives, and it is planted in our heart by God to cause us to follow after our dreams. Desire directs our lives and propels us toward our God-given destiny. Ephesians 1:11–12 says, "*In him* we were also chosen, having been predestined according to the plan of him who works out everything in conformity with the purpose of his will, in order that we, who were the first to hope in Christ, might be for the praise of his glory."

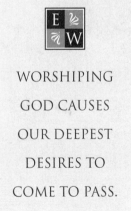

WORSHIPING
GOD CAUSES
OUR DEEPEST
DESIRES TO
COME TO PASS.

Do you know what you were born to do? Have you given definition to that desire that is within you? Have you allowed that desire to breathe—to find the life it needs in order to be realized? Many people struggle with knowing what it is they were born to do, and sometimes they make it too complicated. God doesn't make our "calling" hard, we do!

Ask yourself these things: *What am I gifted at? What do I love to do? Does this desire line up with the Word of God? Can I see it for my life? Will the purpose of my desire build the kingdom of God?*

For many years in my early Christian walk, I tried so hard to say no to the desire deep inside of me to be involved in worship music. I loved playing, singing, and writing music, but I thought perhaps I loved it all too much. I struggled over whether or not I had the character it takes to say no to personal ambition in favor of building something far greater than I could fathom—the kingdom of God.

GOD IS THE ULTIMATE DREAM GIVER AND DREAM FULFILLER.

Until I learned to delight myself in Him, my desire as a musician was there, but I was basically waiting for a break with no clear direction. Week by week, month by month, I learned to trust in God—not in man or programs, but in God, the Creator of heaven and earth. As He lovingly corrected me, faithfully ministered to me, and gently guided me back on the path to His purpose for me, I discovered that He really did have my heart. I wanted to worship Him with all that was within me.

With that powerful understanding, I have seen God's hand literally cause influence in my life. That increase has been in far greater ways than mere musical opportunities. It has come in the form of confidence, anointing, gifting, ability, and new wings to my dreams and desires. That increase has required diligence, discipline, and acceptance of His grace.

God is the ultimate dream giver and dream fulfiller. He planted His dream within you to get you up in the morning. He planted it so that you would go over mountains and through valleys. The Enemy is a dream stealer, and I know that many people feel like some of their dream has been stolen. To live without a dream is to live without a future—"Where there is no vision, the people perish" (Proverbs 29:18 KJV). God wants to restore your dream.

I once heard Tommy Barnett say, "If your dream is too big, then it must be from God." If your dream is not too big for you, then you don't need God to fulfill it! If your dream is enormous, and you think that it cannot possibly be for your life, I guarantee that it is a God dream. The Holy Spirit wants to breathe on your dreams. Perhaps you have dreams that circumstances of life have "put a lid on," keeping them contained to the "impossible" pile. But God will lift that lid and allow you to dream again as you worship Him.

A DREAM BIRTHED

I believe I was born to bring a new song to the house of God. I never believed it at first; it was only a dream, but every now and again I get a glimpse of my dream coming true from deep inside of me. At the age of fifteen, when I became a Christian through the Royal Rangers youth program, the seed of the dream in my heart was planted. I still remember clearly going to the church after I had made that decision. I remember the song that I heard sung that night at church: "I hear the sound of the army of the Lord; I hear the sound of the army of the Lord; it's the sound of praise and it's the sound of war; the army of the Lord is marching on."

They sang it, and they sang it, and they sang it again. I watched the Scriptures come to life as the congregation gathered in the name of Jesus and sang with one voice and in one accord. With my very young fifteen-year-old ears, I heard a new sound that night. My ears had been accustomed to music, but I heard the sound of the army of the Lord starting to rise.

From that day the seed of a dream was planted in me. The reason I was born was planted in me. And from that moment to this I have discovered the truth of the words spoken to Esther: "Yet who knows whether you have come to the kingdom for such a time as this?" (Esther 4:14 NKJV).

I don't know what age you were when the seed of your dream was planted, but I am confident that God has planted it within you. Otherwise you wouldn't be reading this book. There was a time when the seed of your dream was planted in you, but perhaps somewhere along that time line it has been buried. I am so thankful for the Holy Spirit, who has continually drawn me back to the dream He put within me. Gently He would call, "No, no, no. Come back here; stop doing your own thing; come back here and let me fan that dream, because you were born for this purpose."

I heard Him calling me in my spirit; I didn't hear His voice with my natural ears. Do you remember when you heard Him for the first time? When you first heard the new sound of worship? You didn't hear it with your ears; you heard it with your spirit. You heard it in the deepest part of you, where only God can fill. All these years later I hear a similar song rising from the army of the Lord around every nation, tribe, and tongue. God is restoring the song of the Lord to its rightful place. He is calling in the musicians, saying, "Come and take your place." He is calling in the singers: "Come and sing my song; come and do the thing you were born for." He is calling us all to worship: "Come and let the dream that I planted in you live."

I have written my dream down, and the only reason it changes is that it keeps growing! It is a great thing for you to do, to "write down the revelation and make it plain on tablets so that a herald may run with it" (Habakkuk 2:2). Not my dream, *your* dream. Writing down my dream is not going to help you at all, but writing down your dream will.

One of the things that I wrote down as part of my dream is that I will have a major part to play in changing not only the face but also the heart of every worshiper in every church on the planet. That I will have a major part to play in training the most excellent worship teams ever with the most excellent songwriters that have ever graced heaven with a song. I want to train worship teams that have a revelation of the power of praise and worship. My dream is that God's army of worshipers will no longer struggle with the call of God on their lives but will stand strong in His purpose. I want to have a part to play in changing hearts, pointing people to Christ with every step they take, every breath they breathe. That's just a little bit of my dream.

Before I surrendered my gift to use for God's glory, I sang in many places and on many projects that I am not proud of. The opportunities left me empty and unfulfilled. I earned great money, but I wasn't content, because God had birthed in me a bigger dream. He placed me on this earth to be a worshiper of the King of Kings. I'm not condemning those who use their gifts elsewhere. It's just that for me, deep down, I knew I wasn't fulfilling my destiny. I love all music, but music without a kingdom purpose leaves me empty, because I want to use my life to exalt the name of Christ and to take people to the awesome love of God.

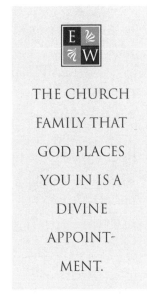

THE CHURCH FAMILY THAT GOD PLACES YOU IN IS A DIVINE APPOINTMENT.

God is the ultimate dream fulfiller, but I had a definite part to play. I had to make good choices along the way. Each time I did, God allowed me to see a little bit of my dream. And a lot of good people chastened me when I made bad choices. I am telling you this because I want you to succeed in life and to see your dream come to pass.

The greatest thing that I have in my life, apart from Jesus and apart from my family, is our worship team and local church family. The church family that God places you in is a divine appointment. When Mark and I started going to Hillsong Church, I was not at all pliable. I tried to enter the worship team on my own terms. Eventually I just backed out of the team because it was all too hard.

Commitment to a team requires dying to self, and I fought it. I did all sorts of things *with* the team. I would do a special Christmas Spectacular show. I would do an item if they needed me, but I wasn't committed to be a team member. At the same time, God knew that in order for me to see the dream in me come to pass that He had birthed and that He was tending to, I had to die to all selfish ambitions. I continually needed to do this so that I could be part of the team that would allow my dream to surface.

I love our worship team. It doesn't seem to change a lot, but it certainly grows. After years of being together, the same core people are still there. We have lost only a few members of the team to other appointments of ministry over the years, which I think is amazing. That is a testimony to the greatness of God and how His discipline on our lives is for our benefit so that He can see His dream in us fulfilled. You can see your dream become a reality in life through being a part of a kingdom team. In life, in a team, the church family is critical.

> *"For I know the plans I have for you," declares the Lord, "plans to prosper you and not to harm you, plans to give you hope and a future"* (Jeremiah 29:11).

We have a prayer that we pray for all the people we see—people in all different parts of the world, people we've never met before, and people we will never see again, who have come to one of the Hillsong worship nights. It is a prayer that we first prayed in a beautiful church in the United States, where people were excited that we were there. Our team agreed this prayer together: *Father, let them quickly get their eyes off of us. We just want to point them to you, God, because you are the Author of truth. You are the only One who is to be praised.* We were so desperate to point people to Christ.

Once we were in an awesome church that practiced a very different style of worship to what we bring. There are many different styles and methods of worship, and all glorify God as long as there is a heart connection between the worshiper and the Lord. But I remember seeing this particular pastor sitting in the front row of his church, and he looked a bit nervous. I think he was really glad he invited us, until we got there and started rehearsing! The church was quite traditional (and quite magnificent as well), and our presence was like the North meeting the South. We walked in, greeted everyone with our Australian accents, and started the sound check. Then I watched the color drain from the pastor's face.

When we visit a church, we can try to tone down what we do to a degree (adjust volumes, etc., to honor the leadership), but in the end I have to give it my all. It's all or nothing. I can't fake it. I have tried, and I'm not good at it. I have to give it my all. What else can I do? The only expression I can give Him is me. That's all I can do, and I am just so in love with the King, I just have to show Him. I have to give Him my all.

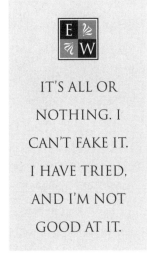

IT'S ALL OR NOTHING. I CAN'T FAKE IT. I HAVE TRIED, AND I'M NOT GOOD AT IT.

So there we were, and we started playing a praise song, and I saw again the worried look on this poor man. I thought, *Jesus, please just take him now, because it is going to be too hard.* We started with praise songs, and by the time we got to worship, this man was standing there with his eyes shut tight. I think he was too scared to open them!

But I saw the moment when this pastor turned around and looked at his church, and people everywhere stood with their hands raised, tears streaming down their faces, as they were just lost in loving their King. He turned back around and burst into tears. This beautiful man, with a burning passion to see people in love with Jesus, had never seen his church love God in that way. Part of his dream was fulfilled that day—as was mine.

That day God reminded me of my dream. He said to me, *"Remember that dream that you would be involved in turning not only the face but also the heart of the church, not just one style of church but the body of Christ, to see God's people become worshipers in spirit and in truth? Worshipers rising up like a mighty army and taking this world for Jesus?!"*

IT DOESN'T MATTER
WHERE YOU START

To see your dream come true, it doesn't matter where you start. Look at the life of David; he didn't have a big illustrious start. Look at the life of Moses: he stuttered and said, "I c-c-can't." He didn't have a great start. I look at my own life. It was not a remarkable start either. It was not a grand opening. It doesn't matter where you start. What *does* matter is that you allow the Holy Spirit to stir up that dream within you so that you can finish your race well.

Steve McPherson is one of the worship leaders in our church. Steve has two brothers who are also magnificent in the field of the arts. They are all magnificent! They are brilliant! The three of them are musical geniuses, yet both of their parents are deaf. Who would have thought? Two deaf parents with three musical geniuses; because the Spirit of God was birthed in them to get up and cause a nation to sing in Jesus' name. That is the faithfulness of God. It doesn't matter where you start.

Trust God's Timing

You can have a dream, and you might be the most faithful person on the planet, but you may still wonder why you are not seeing your dream come to pass. Time is the greatest proving ground for a dream. That can be a hard lesson to learn, because you've been hanging in there, you've been serving, and now you're asking, "When is this dream going to come about?"

Don't stop being faithful in what you are doing. God's timing is perfect. If it is God's dream, it obviously needs time as the perfecting ingredient. God's people, the church, are a magnificent people. Extravagant worshipers are shaking the planet! That's why the Enemy hates worshipers. He hates us. We're not afraid of him; we are full of faith for the future and full of faith for what God is doing through people like you.

Time—don't do all the "sowing in tears" and then leave early! Hang out, for your reaping will be in joy!

Our God Is Able

God enables your "unableness." If you say, "I am unable to fulfill my dream," then God says, "Awesome!" because He "is able to do immeasurably more than all we ask or imagine, according to his power that is at work within us" (Ephesians 3:20). That is what God is saying to you about your dream today.

In Judges 6:11–14, we read the story of Gideon:

> *The angel of the Lord came and sat down under the oak in Ophrah that belonged to Joash the Abiezrite, where his son Gideon was threshing wheat in a winepress to keep it from the Midianites.*
> *When the angel of the Lord appeared to Gideon, he said, "The Lord is with you, mighty warrior."*
> *"But sir," Gideon replied, "if the Lord is with us, why has all this happened to us? Where are all his wonders that our fathers told us about when they said, 'Did not the Lord bring us up out of Egypt?'*

But now the Lord has abandoned us and put us
into the hand of Midian."
The Lord turned to him and said,
"Go in the strength you have and save Israel out of Midian's hand.
Am I not sending you?"

Have you ever felt like Gideon? Have you ever felt abandoned in your dreams? This is what God is saying to you today: "Go—am I not sending you? Do you not believe me? Have you not read my Word? Do you not know what power I hold in my hand? Do you not know that the same Spirit that raised Christ from the dead dwells in you? Do you not know that I am sending you?"

I love the story of Gideon. There he is, with God giving him this amazing promise that He is sending him, and Gideon says, "But Lord, how can I save Israel? My clan is the weakest in Manasseh, and I am the least in my family" (Judges 6:15). Do his excuses sound like yours sometimes?

But the Lord was patient with Gideon and answered, "I will be with you, and you will strike down all the Midianites together" (v. 16).

Then Gideon replied, "If now I have found favor in your eyes, give me a sign that it is really you talking to me" (v. 17).

How funny is that? Gideon is standing right there with the angel of the Lord giving him a message from God (what more do you need), and Gideon says, "I need another sign, just to make sure!" Does this sound like you at all? I know it sounds like me!

Then Gideon said, "Please do not go away until I come back and bring my offering and set it before you." And our beautiful Lord responded, "I will wait until you return" (v. 18).

Most people put their dream on the shelf because they're too scared and too focused on their own inabilities. But God says, "Go in the strength you have—am I not sending you?" If God has placed the dream in you, and God has placed the call on you, has he not equipped you to fulfill that call? He has equipped you! God is sending you! He has put that call on your life. He has given you the gifts to fulfill that call, and that is what you are going to do.

Don't let your dream die because you think you can't achieve it. Let your dream be brought to the surface again. I pray that whatever has veiled your dream, whatever has locked it up within you, that you allow the Holy Spirit to breathe on that seed in your heart so that the brilliance of the dream within has the opportunity to shine.

"Am I not sending you?"

PEARLS AND GOLD

PEARLS AND GOLD
RICHES OF MEN
CAN'T COMPARE TO WHAT I HAVE IN YOU
I STAND IN AWE YOUR BEAUTY TO BEHOLD
YOUR LOVE FOR ME
SO RICH AND SO PURE
I STAND ON HOLY GROUND
CREATE IN ME A HEART OF WORSHIP
JESUS, SAVIOR OF MY SOUL
CREATE IN ME A HEART OF WORSHIP

1993 DARLENE ZSCHECH
HILLSONG PUBLISHING

PART TWO

THE
EXCELLENT
Worshiper

Chapter Six

EXCELLENCE
MATTERS

EXCELLENCE MATTERS

Then make my joy complete by being like-minded, having the same love, being one in spirit and purpose. (Philippians 2:2)

On the night that our worship team recorded the album "You Are My World," I glanced around me and saw the realized potential of a powerful group of extravagant worshipers. Seeing these individuals standing together as strong testimonies to the grace of God, and working toward one common goal, caused tears to fall down my face. I closed my eyes and thanked God from the bottom of my heart that He planted me in this team of worshipers, for I love each one of them dearly. The awesomeness of God's plan takes my breath away.

I believe that there are a few character traits that signify the excellence that individuals in this team bring to their worship. Their excellence dares to press forward and represent the Savior and King. The disciples whom Jesus chose to have around Him were an imperfect bunch of people to spread the Gospel to the ends of the earth. But all of them (most of them) loved Jesus more than life, and that is the challenge of excellence that I lay before all members of the church.

THE DISCIPLES WHOM JESUS CHOSE TO HAVE AROUND HIM WERE AN IMPERFECT BUNCH OF PEOPLE TO SPREAD THE GOSPEL TO THE ENDS OF THE EARTH.

KNOWING CHRIST MATTERS

Most agree that loving Christ more than life is a basic premise to our faith, but we easily get caught up in the busyness of our lives, and this foundational need to love Jesus more than all else isn't everyone's reality. But giving the Lord first place in our lives is absolutely necessary in our worship of Him. We need to continually review our priorities all the time and understand the sovereignty of God on our lives.

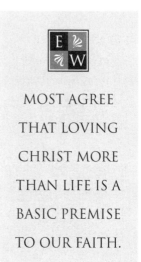

MOST AGREE THAT LOVING CHRIST MORE THAN LIFE IS A BASIC PREMISE TO OUR FAITH.

What a story Job had to tell about priorities in life! Everything that belonged to him was taken away and yet he said, "I know that my Redeemer lives" (Job 19:25). Amen! May we all be able to proclaim, "I know that my Redeemer lives!"

Where would you be without Jesus Christ? You need to know the answer to this question before you bring your gift of worship to the altar. *Know God. Trust in Him.* Know that He lives and know that His heart for you is greater than even your own ambitions for yourself.

YOUR TESTIMONY MATTERS

The worship that you bring to the Lord is fueled by your testimony. Be assured that your testimony matters. My life is a testimony of the grace of God. He is my *everything.* He has done so many miracles in my life that I could tell you stories for months! The Enemy told me I was nothing, saying, "Loser, loser, loser . . ." But God picked me up and said, "No, Darlene. You are a winner, winner, winner! You are a child of God. You are an awesome woman of God."

Your testimony, your personal experiences with God, will bring passion to your gift of worship. If you play an instrument, remembering what God has done for you will cause you to play like you have never played before. If you act, remembering your testimony will enable you to do a street drama and communicate with unsaved people like never before. A personal encounter with God brings a powerful conviction on others because they can see what God has done in you. Your testimony matters.

I sing, and I count the cost of proclaiming my testimony. I live under His authority, and I die daily to my own schedule because of what Christ has done for me. He has done so much for me that I only want to see His name lifted high. I want to see God made famous around the planet. Because He lives, I now have true life.

I have written a new song about living under the "Kiss of Heaven," because I feel like we are caught in the smack of a kiss from God. When we worship Him and live for Him, we are that close to Him—we are living right in His favor, the kiss of heaven. God is kissing His people and saying, "Yes, child, go for it. Go for the dream I've planted in your heart. I am sending you."

EXCELLENCE MATTERS

We are to serve God with excellence because we know an excellent God. To give Him anything but our best would be demeaning. Offer Him your finest, at whatever stage your finest is. Not what you want your finest to be or what you wish it was, but offer your finest for *today*. The testimony and impact of serving with excellence is like watching the ripple effect over the ocean—excellence sends out waves, touching lives in ways that you may never see.

The Word says, "Sing to him a new song; *play skillfully,* and shout for joy" (Psalm 33:3). We are to be skillful in our service to the Lord. I love seeing unsaved people walk into a church where believers have developed skill in their gifted areas for service. When the music is superb, the art is breathtaking; when the givers are giving, the servers are serving, singers are singing, and everyone is worshiping God with his or her unique gift, then visitors stand in awe and say, "Are you serious? Is this church? This is fantastic!"

INCORRECT PERCEPTIONS OF WHAT CHURCH IS OR MEMORIES OF WHAT CHURCH WAS LIKE IN THE PAST HAVE KEPT ALMOST AN ENTIRE GENERATION OUT OF THE HOUSE OF GOD.

Incorrect perceptions of what church is or memories of what church was like in the past have kept almost an entire generation out of the house of God. We are the generation to change that poor image of church. We are to bring excellence back into the sanctuary. We are to loose creativity and put reverence back in the church.

Excellence means *detail*. The crowd can do things well, but the children of the living God should be able to bring "the extraordinary" in to all they do. Excellence means banning the response of "that will do" and "near enough is good enough" from our vocabularies. That mentality will never bring anything outstanding to the sanctuary of the Lord. When the Lord designed the Tabernacle He was meticulous in detail. Exodus 35:35 says, "He has filled them with skill to do all kinds of work as craftsmen, designers, embroiderers in blue, purple and scarlet yarn and fine linen, and weavers—all of them master craftsmen and designers."

Excellence means *discipline*. We need discipline to settle only for what is excellent in our thinking, in our rehearsals, in our personal planning, and in keeping our word to others. The Word says, "Finally, brothers, whatever is true, whatever is noble, whatever is right, whatever is pure, whatever is lovely, whatever is admirable—if anything is excellent or praiseworthy—think about such things" (Philippians 4:8). When our thoughts are excellent, our deeds will be excellent too. And excellence matters.

SERVICE MATTERS

Deuteronomy 10:12–13 says, "And now, O Israel, what does the Lord your God ask of you but to fear the Lord your God, to walk in all his ways, to love him, to *serve the Lord your God with all your heart and with all your soul,* and to observe the Lord's commands and decrees that I am giving you today for your own good?" (emphasis added). Be an extravagant worshiper who is dedicated to serving Him. In the secular world, music and the arts is an exclusive arena. Only a chosen few, a small percentage of people, get past all the auditions; only the people who are highly skilled, who are very beautiful, "get a break" in the music and art world. In the kingdom of God, art and music is inclusive to everyone. God welcomes all to share their artistic gift to express themselves. God says, "You fit into my masterpiece. You belong here!"

There are many musicians who sit alone in their bedrooms night after night, guitar in hand, playing very well, who wish someone could hear them other than themselves. If only they would dedicate their God-given talent to His service. God is calling the highly skilled musicians to dedicate their music to the service of the King. Serving Him brings a joy that cannot be found outside of His purpose. One can find money and plenty of it outside of serving the Lord, but indescribable joy accompanies service to the King.

Every year in July we host the Hillsong Conference, and thousands of people come from all over the world to learn leadership skills for all areas of service. The mission of the conference is to equip people and champion the cause of the local church. My heart swells just thinking about this awesome opportunity!

When Mark and I read the feedback forms from the conference, the overwhelming majority of people don't comment on how wonderful the music was, the songs, or the preaching. It's not the worship leaders or the choir that impresses the conferees. The majority of people who review the conference are "blown away" by the level of commitment from the church team and by the joyful fruit of their dedicated service.

Visitors to our conferences are impressed by the person standing in the rain to help them park their cars and get into the meeting quickly. They mention the young Bible college student who volunteered sixteen hours a day for a week so that people could come to the conference and be blessed. They mention the young girl who gave up attending the conference and spent the week working in the nursery so that others could be ministered to. These skilled workers *volunteered* because of their commitment to serving the Lord.

UNITY MATTERS

Unity not only matters, it's essential. Unity in the church is very critical to the testimony of the church. Jesus prayed for unity among all believers, saying,

> *I do not ask in behalf of these alone, but for those also who believe in Me*
> *through their word; that they may all be one; even as Thou, Father, art*
> *in Me, and I in Thee, that they also may be in Us; that the*
> *world may believe that Thou didst send Me.*
> *And the glory which Thou hast given Me I have given to them; that they*
> *may be one, just as We are one; I in them, and Thou in Me, that they*
> *may be perfected in unity, that the world may know that Thou didst*
> *send Me, and didst love them, even as Thou didst love Me.*
> *(John 17:20–23* NASB*)*

Unity supernaturally shows the world that God sent Jesus to demonstrate His love to us. This truth needs to sink deep into our spirits, allow-ing unity to flow through the church so that the world may know Him. Psalm 133:1 says, "How good and pleasant it is when brothers live together in unity!"

"May the God who gives endurance and encouragement give you a spirit of unity among yourselves as you follow Christ Jesus, so that with one heart and mouth you may glorify the God and Father of our Lord Jesus Christ" (Romans 15:5–6).

God loves unity. What a glorious testimony to His goodness it is when His worshipers laugh together, pray together, minister together, get down and do life together. This is a rare and precious thing, and God says that if we dwell in unity He commands blessing. To be in unity is a decision that we must *all* continually make. We even have to fight for it, because the Enemy wants to divide and weaken us.

Do whatever it takes to have and to keep unity, because God blesses it and He responds to it. In fact, He requires unity. The Word says, "Forgive whatever grievances you may have against one another. Forgive as the Lord forgave you. And over all these virtues *put on love, which binds them all together in perfect unity"* (Colossians 3:13–14, emphasis added).

> UNITY SUPER-
> NATURALLY
> SHOWS THE
> WORLD THAT
> GOD SENT
> JESUS TO
> DEMONSTRATE
> HIS LOVE
> TO US.

Ephesians 4:11–14 says that God gave us various gifts to help build one another up: "Until we all reach unity in the faith and in the knowledge of the Son of God and become mature, attaining to the whole measure of the fullness of Christ. Then we will no longer be infants, tossed back and forth by the waves, and blown here and there by every wind of teaching and by the cunning and craftiness of men in their deceitful scheming."

Unity can't happen without maturity. God blesses unity, and we can't have unity without growing up spiritually. We pray for unity, which is excellent, but if we don't make an effort to love each other enough to do something radical about it, we won't see the blessing that God wants to pour out on a unified, mature church.

BE COMMITTED TO UNITY AND RECON- CILIATION WITHIN THE CHURCH BODY WHERE GOD HAS PUT YOU.

Be committed to unity and reconciliation within the church body where God has put you. You may not be one of the leaders on the platform, but you are still part of the team, even if you are worshiping from the church pew. Just be committed to the body of Christ that God leads you to. Don't leave a question mark. Don't even leave room for a little crack in the door that lets you out of responsibility. Be committed to your local church team, and do whatever you must to have unity. Lay down your life—lose it so others may find theirs. Do whatever it takes. God honors unity every time He finds it.

Ephesians 4:2–6 says, "Be completely humble and gentle; be patient, bearing with one another in love. Make every effort to keep the unity of the Spirit through the bond of peace. There is one body and one Spirit—just as you were called to one hope when you were called—one Lord, one faith, one baptism; one God and Father of all, who is over all and through all and in all."

"Make every effort" means we actually have to do something. If we pray for unity and yet still hold on to grudges over silly things, the church will never be the head instead of the tail. We must get into our community and say, "We have something to sing about, we have something to live for; our God is an awesome God, and He has asked us to 'do life' with people from diverse backgrounds. And look at us, we actually love each other and are committed to one another, and it is a great testimony!"

Unity does not come by chance; it does not come without work, and it does not come without dying to self on a daily basis. It is hard sometimes, but it is so worth it. It's time for God's people to *grow up*!

FRIENDSHIP MATTERS

Genuine friendship matters among believers. The Word says we are to offer more than is asked of us. We're to imitate Christ to others. We're to offer the type of friendship that takes a blow for someone even when it costs us. We are to be the friend that lays down his life for another—that is a serious friendship. When Jesus gathered His friends the disciples for their final Passover meal, He said, "I have *eagerly desired* to eat this Passover with you" (Luke 22:15, emphasis added).

I can honestly say from my heart that I eagerly desire to be with the people in our worship team. God has not only called us to play music together but He has also called us to be ministers of His holy Word together. We should have strong friendships with those who worship with us. But I admit our friendships with each other have required a choice and commitment. Imagine getting ten to twenty people in a worship team—all creative, passionate, emotional people! And God says, "I am going to use all of your strengths and all of your weaknesses, and I am going to pull you together to minister in my courts and to lead people to me." Wow! That is a *big* calling. But serving God with my friends is probably one of the secret bonuses I never expected to find in this journey of discovery.

EXTREME GENEROSITY MATTERS

The Christmas story of the wise men coming to Bethlehem to adore their King is a beautiful account of worship. These brave men traveled many miles to bring their "personal treasures" and set their gifts before the Savior of the world. When they saw the Christ child, they were filled with joy and they fell down in worship. They opened what they had brought for Him and gave their generous gifts of gold, frankincense, and myrrh because they were so in love with the King.

Matthew 6:21 says, "For where your treasure is, there your heart will be also." Your treasure is the thing that you hold the closest to you, but these men were so thankful that Christ was born that they opened their personal treasure and gave to Him out of it. They would never forget the day their Savior was born. As I was reading that story, I could almost see all of heaven smiling as the angels sang, "Hallelujah!" The account of their long trip and their extreme generosity has been told for two thousand years to all mankind.

AN EXTRAVAGANT WORSHIPER HAS A GENEROUS HEART EVEN OUTSIDE THE SANCTUARY.

An extravagant worshiper has a generous heart even outside the sanctuary. Be generous in your love toward one another. Look for ways that you can go outside of yourself, outside of your comfort zone, to be generous. Do something that really blesses someone, something that costs you, even if only a few cents to post a letter. Send a thank-you card to someone who's been doing great work behind the scenes, or even to someone who's always seen working hard. It doesn't cost much money to recognize someone with appreciation. Extreme generosity doesn't require a million-dollar contribution. Surprise someone with a random act of kindness.

If we can stand in the sanctuary and praise the Lord with our glorious song, we should also serve Him with extravagant love for others, or else something is wrong with our life's message. Be generous in your worship both inside and outside the sanctuary. Proverbs 11:25 says, "A generous man will prosper; he who refreshes others will himself be refreshed." And Proverbs 22:9 says, "A generous man will himself be blessed, for he shares his food with the poor."

I am not talking about simply giving money; I am talking about letting generosity be part of who you are. I believe that if we dare to call ourselves extravagant worshipers, we ought to be leaders in everything, not just music, and being extremely generous is part of the result of spending time in the presence of God. Generosity is a key to unlocking the windows of blessing on our lives. We are to give from a heart that doesn't only want to receive but that gives because we love Him more than our life. Mark 8:35 says, "For whoever wants to save his life will lose it, but whoever loses his life for me and for the gospel will save it." An extravagant worshiper will want to give his or her life for the Gospel—

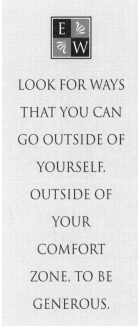

LOOK FOR WAYS THAT YOU CAN GO OUTSIDE OF YOURSELF, OUTSIDE OF YOUR COMFORT ZONE, TO BE GENEROUS.

that is extreme generosity. Generous describes the core of who Jesus is.

DISCIPLINE AND DETERMINATION MATTER

As extravagant worshipers, we need to overrule our feelings. Worship releases creativity in us, but creative people tend to live in the "feelings" department. This tendency can be both our best and our worst feature. Feelings can bring us to brilliant conclusions, but they can also destroy us if we don't place our feelings under submission to God's Word. Isaiah 50:4–7 says,

IF WE CAN GET UP

ON THE PLATFORM,

AND IF WE CAN PRAISE HIM

WITH OUR GLORIOUS SONG,

BUT WE CAN'T SERVE HIM

WITH EXTRAVAGANT LIVES,

THEN SOMETHING IS WRONG

WITH OUR MESSAGE.

The Sovereign Lord has given me an instructed tongue, to know the word that sustains the weary. He wakens me morning by morning, wakens my ear to listen like one being taught.
The Sovereign Lord has opened my ears, and I have not been rebellious; I have not drawn back. I offered my back to those who beat me, my cheeks to those who pulled out my beard; I did not hide my face from mocking and spitting. Because the Sovereign Lord helps me, I will not be disgraced. Therefore have I set my face like flint, and I know I will not be put to shame.

I love these Scriptures because they show us how to have determination. "I will *not* be tossed. I will *not* be moved. I will *not* draw back." We must be *determined* to grab hold of God and ask for our miracle, because He is *more* desperate to pour His glory on us than we are to receive it! We need determination to complete our mission. As an extravagant worshiper, we are never on a "gig" or a "show." We are on a heavenly mission, and being determined to see His purposes accomplished requires a response from our glorious God.

Discipline your mind to agree with God's Word. It will affect your speech, and it will affect your attitude toward excellence. It will affect your attitude—period! I love the story in Daniel where Shadrach, Meshach, and Abednego are in the fiery furnace, and they *know* their God will save them. In the middle of a fire (big trial) I can just hear them say, "We're *not* bowing, we're praising God. So you can throw us in the fire, you can put us in the lion's den, you can do whatever you want, and we are just going to praise our God, because we are fearfully and wonderfully made. We are rejoicing in the Lord always, and we are going to continue to bless His name at all times. His praise will continually be in our mouths." They were extravagant worshipers together.

But their determination was evident when they agreed, "But even if he does not [deliver us], we want you to know, O king, that we will not serve your gods or worship the image of gold you have set up" (Daniel

3:18). It takes that sort of determination, that sort of discipline, to follow through with the call of God on your life.

Sometimes it might not *feel* like everything you need is there in front of you. But if you are in a valley of despair and discouragement, you need to know God intimately enough to say, "Even in the midst of this, I will *not* bow. I know my God and I know His heart for me, so if I am in a valley, Lord, let me learn; let me learn quickly." Learn this lesson of determination quickly, otherwise this test of faith will come right back at you again until you do learn it. Be determined with that fire in your belly that says, "I will bless the Lord at all times, all times and in all ways."

Whatever gift or treasure you bring to the altar, cover it with the determination and discipline to bless the Lord no matter what. Know God intimately through personal worship so you will know that He is faithful. Know He oversees His call on your life to fulfill His work. Don't worry about it. Just serve Him and be glad.

BE STRONG

Extravagant worshipers know how to be lovers of God, and they become a pillar of strength. We are created in the image of God. Be strong in unity, excellence, determination, and service. All these things matter and reflect an exceptional attitude as one who has spent time in the presence of the Lord.

Don't be afraid of discipline, both in the mind—which is thinking right—and in action—which is living right. Proverbs 10:17 says, "He who heeds discipline shows the way to life, but whoever ignores correction leads others astray." Proverbs 1:7 says, "But fools despise wisdom and discipline." And Proverbs 13:18: "He who ignores discipline comes to poverty and shame, but whoever heeds correction is honored." Don't be afraid of discipline.

If you are enjoying a season of favor and success, I challenge you not to lose sight of the discipline and faithfulness that placed you there. Success is a challenge for an extravagant worshiper because success is one of our greatest enemies. Worship brings favor and success into our lives, but success can give us a false sense of how great we are. We can quickly forget that our success is the result of how great God is.

Success can tempt you to ride on its momentum rather than continue to do the faithful things that allowed you to walk that path in the first place. I challenge you not to refrain from doing all those things that allow you the privilege of having influence, no matter how great or small. Keep worship of the Lord first and foremost in your life.

After a few years of leading worship in our church, I changed singing teachers, purely because I heard this woman was the best there was. In fact, I heard she was fantastic, and I was really excited about my first lesson. I prepared a song to show her what I could do, and I sat at the piano and began to play and sing "Let It Be" by the Beatles. When I had finished, there was silence, so I just turned around and waited. I was really anxious to hear her comments, and I thought I had done okay.

You can imagine my embarrassment when she slammed the lid down on the piano and said, "That is the biggest load of _____

IF YOU ARE ENJOYING A SEASON OF FAVOR AND SUCCESS, I CHALLENGE YOU NOT TO LOSE SIGHT OF THE DISCIPLINE AND FAITHFULNESS THAT PLACED YOU THERE.

I have ever heard!" She then proceeded to say, "You are a church singer, aren't you? You have had an army of people around you for years encouraging you, and you have stopped working on your gift."

It was a horrible day, but I received the lesson—she was right. In our encouraging church environment, it is easy to taste a small amount of success and develop a false sense of how good we really are. To add insult to injury, this singing teacher later took me into a vocal symposium to show people how *not* to sing!

Success can make us slack and casual; it can make us presumptuous that "everything will be all right." We stop worrying about rehearsal; "worship will be great." Well, it won't be if we don't keep practicing faith throughout the week. Worship won't be great if we don't make it different from the service before. It won't be if we don't know the songs!

Don't presume that you can bring casual gifts to worship. "Only fools despise wisdom and discipline." Keep your attention on the details; keep that fire in your being, that attitude of "whatever it takes." Keep the zeal in your worship that drove you to God's face when you first believed. Go back to that place where the call of God drove you crazy, to that call of God from which you could not escape. Don't fear discipline and faithfulness, because they can be your greatest friends.

THE POWER AND THE PITFALLS OF SUCCESS

Do not let this Book of the Law depart from your mouth; meditate on it day and night, so that you may be careful to do everything written in it. Then you will be prosperous and successful. (Joshua 1:8)

Every Christian has the desire to be successful and to achieve God's purposes for his or her life. Yet why do many taste success and remain unfulfilled? The pursuit of success for the sake of being successful is an empty well. Success in itself will not satisfy us. The world's picture of success is so seductive: it offers money, fame, and glamour. Yet God's picture of success is that of a servant, dead to self and alive to Christ. I believe success can be both a positive and a negative influence, and it's your choice which road of success you will walk.

Success Generates Momentum

The momentum of success can be your best friend—it's like the breath of God, making one day to be more valuable and worthwhile than a thousand days. When momentum is on your side, the future looks bright, obstacles look small, and troubles seem transitory. Momentum actually makes you look better than you are.

You can abuse momentum if you stop digging for the gold that gave it to you in the first place. If you stop pursuing the basics of faith, the core values of love, you will lose the favor that first brought success. We're simply to seek the kingdom of God and His righteousness, peace, and joy in the Holy Ghost. If we do, success will inevitably follow. But if you take your eyes off of the kingdom of heaven and begin to think, *I'm awesome; we're awesome; we can do it!* you will abuse the privilege of success and lose sight of the higher call.

Success Brings Focus

When people are focused, they develop a sense of destiny and purpose and start to believe in themselves. Suddenly destiny is attainable, focus is sharpened, and they develop that "iron will" or determination in their souls. This is an awesome place to be!

If we don't focus on the right thing, we are in trouble. There's a temptation to focus on the gift instead of the gift giver. That is dangerous ground. This leads to strife, comparison, discontentment, greed, and jealousy. Don't go there! Keep your eyes on the prize; focus your efforts outward rather than inward. Focus on the Lord and not only on all His benefits.

With Success Comes Influence

What an honor it is to have influence! God, through His incredible grace, has given us favor to influence godly changes in people's lives. To be a part of building God's kingdom is so exciting!

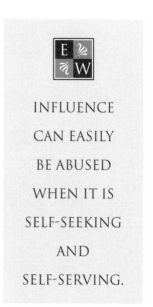

INFLUENCE CAN EASILY BE ABUSED WHEN IT IS SELF-SEEKING AND SELF-SERVING.

Influence can easily be abused when it is self-seeking and self-serving. Many people have been a part of great ministry teams and then suddenly believed that the success was all about them and that their team was holding them back. This thinking causes people to lose the humility that gave them that influence in the first place! Many people crave influence and fame, but they aren't prepared to pay the price or take on the responsibility that goes hand in hand with that influence.

It takes guts to be an influence for the kingdom of God. Many people are content to simply sit in the crowd, because they don't want to be seen. They don't want to be noticed, because with influence comes the responsibility of leading people to a godly place. God wants worshipers who are not just part of the crowd but who will stand out from the crowd.

God isn't looking for someone who is amazingly talented to influence others to live a godly life; He looks for someone who will be obedient. God uses ordinary people like you and me. Any influence I have is only because God has put it in my hand. I love the King, and I want to love Him more than my life. But I've learned that it takes courage to be an influence, because I must be willing to stand out from the crowd. I can't hide my faith or my love for Him if I want to continue to be an influence.

I WILL BLESS YOU, LORD

I TRUST IN YOU, MY FAITHFUL LORD
HOW PERFECT IS YOUR LOVE
YOU ANSWER ME BEFORE I CALL,
MY HOPE, MY STRENGTH, MY SONG
AND I SHOUT FOR JOY
I THANK YOU, LORD
YOUR PLAN STANDS FIRM FOREVER
AND YOUR PRAISE WILL BE CONTINUALLY
POURING FROM MY HEART
I WILL BLESS YOU, LORD
I WILL BLESS YOU, LORD
HOW MY SOUL CRIES OUT
FOR YOU, MY GOD
I WILL BLESS YOU, LORD

1997 DARLENE ZSCHECH
HILLSONG PUBLISHING

Success Is Attractive

Like attracts like, and when you walk the path of success with humility, like-hearted people are attracted to you, which forms powerful partnerships. To be part of a team of extravagant worshipers that works together in unity is a great thing; it is something I cherish and never take for granted. A worshiping church attracts worshiping people.

However, if you want to be successful so that you can be seen, then this will also attract like-hearted people. But living for affirmation and approval of others is a tiring way to live. If your self-worth constantly relies on popularity, your success journey is reduced to self-gratification! There is no joy in that fruitless effort.

You Can Walk the Success Road Well

Understand that success in the kingdom of God is all about building the lives of others. Your life purpose is tied somehow to this one cause. Joshua 1:8 teaches us how to walk the road of success well. It says, "Meditate on it [the Word of God] day and night, so that you may be careful to do everything written in it. *Then* you will be prosperous and successful."

Be faithful, faithful, faithful. Be faithful in the small things. Be faithful in the private moments that are unseen. Above all, have a heart that is desperate to see God's purposes established and that beats only to glorify Him. We must not let this great enemy called success tie us in knots and strangle us or pull us back. As extravagant worshipers who dare to press forward and represent the Savior and King, we must not retreat.

Chapter Seven

EDUCATE
THE MIND

EDUCATE
THE MIND

There was a time when I was confused about my role in ministry. I loved the Lord, but I wasn't sure how I fit in to the church life. I loved to sing, and I continually auditioned for bands; I even auditioned for the musical *Hair!* (What was I thinking?) Out of fear, I did whatever I could possibly do to keep from becoming "just a church singer." I though that singing, or bringing one's gift inside the church, had a stigma attached to it, which I now find to be an incredible misgiving. The church is the reason gifts and talents are given to us in the first place! Our gifts are to be used for the glory of God!

I had *no* understanding of what it meant to know my purpose and pursue it with my creative being. I trusted God in other areas, but I was nervous about sowing my musical gift into my local church to further the kingdom of God. I had been performing since I was about three years old. By the time I became a Christian, I had been paid to sing and entertain professionally for five years. My beautiful mother had me singing wherever anyone would watch and listen, even if they really didn't want to!

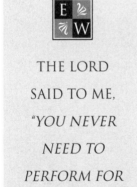

THE LORD
SAID TO ME,
*"YOU NEVER
NEED TO
PERFORM FOR
ME."*

But there was one defining moment, early in my Christian walk, which has kept clarity in my heart and mind about leading worship. I was praying that day to my new Best Friend, when I sensed that still, small voice whisper into the fabric of who I was. The

Lord said to me, *"You never need to perform for me."*

I stopped and thought, *What was that?* I knew it wasn't a thought that I generated myself; I'm not even wired to think like that! I didn't know what the voice of God sounded like! But somehow I knew it was the sweet, kind voice of the Holy Spirit, separating my past from my future, realigning my life with His, and pointing it in the direction that God had preplanned. I pray that as you read this, you too will receive a revelation from God that our salvation is not based on our talents. Salvation is not about how great we are but about how grace-filled our magnificent God is!

It was years later that I started leading worship, but that unmistakable voice whispered that truth into my life again and again. It freed me to lead people without being caught in the trap of being a "worship artist." I was locked into a performance-based Christianity. But His words freed me from my continual effort to be a man pleaser into living a life that exists to be a God pleaser.

Even though I held the key, this word from God, it was still difficult to unlock the pattern of thought that I would somehow need to earn my salvation. My understanding of God's grace was still in its infancy; my progress was held back by doubt and unbelief. What I do and who I am were still unhealthily intertwined for a number of years. This unhealthy thinking is a real problem for so many people. But with time, through reading the Word and through building a *relationship* with God, my mind slowly became renewed.

Renewing the Mind

Hebrews 10:16 says, "I will put my laws in their hearts, and I will write them on their minds." Romans 12:2 says, "Do not conform any longer to the pattern of this world, but be transformed by the renewing of your mind. Then you will be able to test and approve what God's will is—his good, pleasing and perfect will."

I thought it took great discipline to become a singer—practice, warm-ups, etc., but renewing my mind has taken even *greater* discipline! Learning to take *every* thought captive requires stamina. I would take a step forward and start to rise up in the things of God, and then before I realized what was happening, I had taken a step back. But I have learned that I don't have to go through the backward steps if I let the power of the Word of God renew my mind.

If keeping your thoughts in line with God's Word is difficult for you, then I suggest that you listen to teaching tapes. For many years now, my car has been my "renewing your mind" school as I have listened to hundreds of hours of Bible teaching to reeducate my inner man while commuting. To keep your thoughts in line with God's, it is important to carefully choose what to watch on television or listen to on the radio. If you put garbage into your mind, you'll get garbage out.

Feed your mind with the Word of God. Don't starve your mind for knowledge of His truth, or your mind will find something else with which to fill itself. Give your thoughts the right food—feed yourself the truth, and your heart will meditate on God's best for you.

I think it's important to do a heart check on yourself sometimes. Do you speak death or life? It depends on your heart. Do you love gossip, or do you ignore it? It depends on your heart. The power of the tongue is an amazing thing. What you confess over your world is an amazing thing. It has such power. What you feast on will come through as an excellent worshiper or a weak one; feast on

> DON'T STARVE YOUR MIND FOR KNOWLEDGE OF HIS TRUTH, OR YOUR MIND WILL FIND SOMETHING ELSE WITH WHICH TO FILL ITSELF.

the Word and let its transforming power frame your world. Worship is a song of the heart—sooner or later its health will be revealed.

The heart is the engine room of our life. Proverbs 4:23 KJV says, "Keep thy heart with all diligence; for out of it are the issues of life." It's amazing that people spend thousands of dollars, hours and hours a day, exercising their bodies, making themselves feel good and look good. Yet they refuse to spend any time renewing their mind to strengthen their heart—the engine room of life itself.

Psalm 139:13–14 says, "For you created my inmost being; you knit me together in my mother's womb. I praise you because I am fearfully and wonderfully made; your works are wonderful, I know that full well." It took me years to get to the point where I could actually say, "I am wonderfully made and His works are wonderful." Years! It was the process of renewing my mind that enabled me to change my thinking.

God is merciful, and in spite of my doubt and seemingly endless insecurities, He was with me every step of the way. Gently guiding me, like a parent patiently teaching his precious child to walk. Notice how parents say to their child, "Come on, sweetheart, that's it; you are so brilliant!" And when the toddler falls, we clap and say, "Well done! Good try!" We help them stand and go through it all again, cheering them on and helping them up again and again. In our pursuit of Christ and our understanding of His gift of salvation, our precious Father says to us, "That's it; well done! Trust me; I'll catch you!"

In the year 2000 the American Society of Composers, Authors, and Publishers nominated me for songwriter of the year. It was an awesome honor, but on the way to the ceremony I was very, very nervous. As I said earlier, before I was a worship leader I worked in the secular music industry doing gigs and singing jingles for TV ads. So I came from an environment where a great deal of attention is given to self and to gaining recognition for your talent. As a worshiper, I had worked for many years to decrease myself and increase Him. So it made me nervous to walk back into an environment, even though it was a Christian one, where it would be possible to focus on the business of music rather than the reason for the music.

We are all weak, no matter how strong we think we are. We are all able to get it wrong in life, so I was nervous. But on that long plane ride from Sydney to Nashville, the Holy Spirit spoke clearly into my heart and said, "You are not for sale. You have been bought with a price." His words gave me confidence as I walked into that arena of honor, knowing that my affections were truly His.

PRIDE

I take seriously the responsibility of being a worship pastor and a lead worshiper. It's a sobering fact that the only being to get thrown out of heaven was a worship leader! Pride is a seed that can take root *so* easily. God's Word has much to say on this topic:

IT'S A SOBERING FACT THAT THE ONLY BEING TO GET THROWN OUT OF HEAVEN WAS A WORSHIP LEADER!

A man's pride brings him low, but a man of lowly spirit gains honor.
(Proverbs 29:23)
For everything in the world—the cravings of sinful man, the lust of his
eyes and the boasting of what he has and does—comes not from the
Father but from the world. The world and its desires pass away, but the
man who does the will of God lives forever. (1 John 2:16–17)

We must each learn to keep our heart and head in check. One of the great dangers we face at Hillsong is the fact that we have become famous for our worship. But our job is to make God famous in our worship.

Keeping that at the core of our hearts certainly puts everything back into perspective.

One time I was invited to sing at a church here in Australia. When I got there, I was just one of a million things happening on that night. At the end of the evening, because I was an invited guest, I assumed someone would be there to take me to the hotel. So there I was, hanging around the back room. When there were not so many people around anymore, I realized they had not arranged for anyone to take me home!

AS YOU RECEIVE REVELATIONS OF GOD'S LOVE, YOU CAN BEGIN TO THINK THAT YOU DESERVE HIS LOVE AND THEREFORE DESERVE LOVE FROM EVERYONE ELSE TOO!

I didn't know anyone, so I asked a girl if she would drive me to the hotel, and she said no! I ended up paying her to take me. I was so embarrassed to have been so presumptuous. The next morning I hired a taxi to take me to the morning meeting. I sang for them and then got on a plane for home as quickly as possible! So much for thinking I was becoming a "somebody"! I think God arranged the incident to keep my head in order!

Pride is one of the biggest hurdles a musician and singer face, but it is also a potential pitfall for anyone. Paul explains this in his letter to the church at Corinth, saying,

I will not boast about myself, except about my weaknesses. Even if I should choose to boast, I would not be a fool, because I would be speaking the truth.
But I refrain, so no one will think more of me than is warranted by what I do or say.
To keep me from becoming conceited because of these surpassingly great

revelations, there was given me a thorn in my flesh,
a messenger of Satan, to torment me.
Three times I pleaded with the Lord to take it away from me.
But he said to me, "My grace is sufficient for you, for my power
is made perfect in weakness." Therefore I will boast all the more gladly
about my weaknesses, so that Christ's power may rest on me.
(2 Corinthians 12:5–9)

As you receive revelations of God's love, you can begin to think that you deserve His love and therefore deserve love from everyone else too! If you can negate that prideful hurdle, you will release yourself to a great life of service in the kingdom. Not thinking too highly of yourself, preferring others, and listening to advice or correction are all ways that will help you to resist the ugly temptation of pride. So will being part of a team who will say to you, "Hey, buddy, get yourself together! Pull your head in!"

One of our worship leaders, Steve McPherson, was at the airport, where he met a guy who told him he was coming to our church that weekend and that he was a *great* singer and would be awesome on our team. So Steve, as he should, invited him to come to our Wednesday night rehearsal so that he could audition for the choir. The man put up his hand and said, "No, you don't understand. I am a *very, very anointed* singer."

Steve said, "Fantastic, come along and audition for the choir." But the guy never came to the audition, most likely because he could not accept the fact that we wouldn't be featuring his wonderful singing ability that Sunday! If worship is ever more about our talent than about being an excellent worshiper of the living God, then we are in serious trouble.

IT'S A NEW SEASON

"See, I am doing a new thing! Now it springs up; do you not perceive it? I am making a way in the desert and streams in the wasteland.

The wild animals honor me, the jackals and the owls, because I provide water in the desert and streams in the wasteland, to give drink to my people, my chosen, the people I formed for myself that they may proclaim my praise" (Isaiah 43:19–21).

I believe that you and I, as God's people, have only seen a glimpse of the relationship with God that is yet to come in our future. God has whetted our appetite for His glory. The church throughout the earth is taking her rightful place as the beautiful bride of Christ, and we are seeing an increase of God's presence like we have never experienced before. All over the world, people are becoming radical in their pursuit of Christ. We are on the edge of something powerful!

There is a generation of worshipers rising that know the awesome power of His presence and will again bring forth a new song. "Jesus, What a Beautiful Name" was written by a girl in our church, Tanya Riches, at the grand old age of sixteen! And yet I know there will continue to be even younger songwriters who will bring the church to deeper worship. In the future we will be shocked by the age of people from whom new songs come. We will be awed at the depth of character that is about to come forward from our young people. We will be amazed at their prophetic words. *Expect it,* as expectation is the breeding ground of the miraculous.

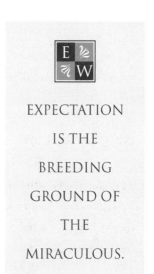

EXPECTATION IS THE BREEDING GROUND OF THE MIRACULOUS.

Dare to stick it out; dare to take your place in this magnificent moment in history. For who knows what is just around the corner? I sense that the water is rising, the spiritual tide is rising, and we are about to experience a mighty crash, like a tidal wave, as our desire to serve Him consumes us. If you want it, it's already there. We are on the brink of something miraculous, so I'm encouraging everyone in the church to get ready. Be big people. It takes guts to be an excellent worshiper. I never want to write the formula for becoming a "successful worshiper." But I do hope to inspire the church to be *radical* for Christ—that is the benchmark I am after.

Once we had so many people coming to our church that on a particular Sunday it was a full forty-five minutes before the service was to start, and people were already coming in. We had people all over the place, and so our senior pastor, Brian Houston, ran past me and said, "We need to have a service—now. You've got twelve minutes till worship."

I think I stopped hearing what he said after that. *Twelve minutes? What's twelve minutes?* So I said to Ian Fisher, one of our music pastors, "We have twelve minutes to take people from chaos (people were everywhere still looking for the nursery and looking for seats) to being aware of the presence of Almighty God." So Ian grabbed the team and said to them, "Right, twelve minutes; you people have been preparing for this all your lives. Now stand in the call of God; go out there, and in twelve minutes we are going to take people to the throne room of God. We are going to give them a taste of heaven. Okay?!" He spoke faith into every one of those excellent worshipers on the team.

We prayed, we got on that platform, and the church did not know what hit them. It was like all of heaven found these praising people too good to be true. The first thirty seconds were truly magnificent. Worship was glorious straight away—you could taste it, you could see it; it was the presence of God, and it resided, it camped. I cannot explain what happened, but within twelve minutes people's lives were turned 180 degrees, and for one hour we had the most magnificent service. We had "out of this world" praise and worship; the Word was preached; we took up an offering, which is part of people's worship; we had a magnificent altar call, and people left; that was one hour, and in the next half hour the next crowd entered, and we started again.

We learned that day that if you have a revelation about the power of praise and worship and are living as a worshiper, you can lead others into the courts of heaven in twelve minutes. We must do more than *hope* somebody will worship; we *have to lead* people. We must take them by the hand and say, "I know that it is tough out there, but let me take you to the answer for your life."

Individuals who become excellent worshipers will find that they will lead others into worship too. Worshiping parents will lead their children into the presence of God. Worshiping neighbors will lead neighbors; worshiping employees will lead their employers into His presence. Excellent worship is contagious.

WORSHIPING PARENTS WILL LEAD THEIR CHILDREN INTO THE PRESENCE OF GOD.

TALENT VS. FAITHFULNESS

Let those who love the Lord hate evil, for he guards the lives of his faithful ones and delivers them from the hand of the wicked.
(Psalm 97:10)

Faithfulness is not a popular word in today's world, but it is a virtue that brings great blessing when applied over any area of our lives. Mark and I have seen firsthand that there is blessing when we are faithful to the cause of Christ. There is blessing when we are faithful to His love. Talent has almost nothing to do with whether or not there is blessing. Your gifts and your talents are God given. And while gifts and talents are sought-after commodities by the world, they are low on God's list of "must haves" to qualify you for living an effective, purpose-driven, Christ-honoring life.

Second Chronicles 16:9 NKJV says, "For the eyes of the Lord run to and fro throughout the whole earth, to show Himself strong on behalf of those whose heart is loyal to Him." We must continually remember that the reason we do what we do is to worship the Lord and to reach souls for His kingdom. If we see the church as an avenue for our gifts, an opportunity, an outlet, a way for people to experience what we have, or a way to success, then we're in the wrong place. Church is not a vehicle for us to present our talents and catapult us into Christian stardom!

At our church, in our worship team, we are up front with people about the issue of seeking fame. The church is all about God and people, and I would rather have the man or the woman of God than the gift. The man and the woman of God come first. There are so many gifted people. It's really not a problem to find someone who is talented; talented people are everywhere. We want to see men and women of God who are fired up with the cause of Christ, and when they play or sing or lead, people are drawn to their knees because of their passion for Christ. There is a remarkable difference between a gifted musician and an anointed one. It is quite easy to discern when someone auditions for the choir simply for the opportunity or when they come to be part of the glorious presence of God. Loyalty and faithfulness are precious commodities when it comes to being an excellent worshiper.

CHURCH IS NOT A VEHICLE FOR US TO PRESENT OUR TALENTS AND CATAPULT US INTO CHRISTIAN STARDOM!

Excellent worshipers need to be steadfast, firm, fixed, constant, reliable, and immovable. Not *re*movable—*im*movable. I'm not going anywhere. I know my call in life; I am here, and I am standing strong. I am not going to be tossed around by the silly things that life would throw at me or that the Enemy would throw at me, but I'm going to be someone who stands on the strength of the Word of God.

RISE TO THE CHALLENGE OF EXCELLENT WORSHIP

I have seen many singers and musicians who wanted to lead worship fall short of their potential because they wouldn't rise to the level of excellence in their own lives that brings the blessing of God. For a time the favor of God seems to cover all sorts of lousy things in our lives, but eventually we must take responsibility for our choices if we want God to trust us with more opportunities. The decision to become the person that Jesus Christ purposed and intended for us to be is ours to make. People can encourage us, motivate us, and build us up, but in the end we must make an individual decision to keep our hearts loyal only to Him.

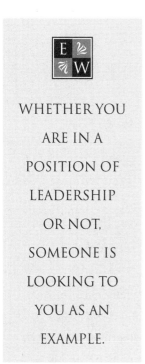

WHETHER YOU ARE IN A POSITION OF LEADERSHIP OR NOT, SOMEONE IS LOOKING TO YOU AS AN EXAMPLE.

I challenge you to be an excellent worshiper both publicly and privately. Whether you are in a position of leadership or not, someone is looking to you as an example. Someone, somewhere, will notice if you are committed to worshiping God or not. Don't give them a musical example. People don't need to follow your talent. Give them a life to follow, a life that radiates God's glory. Live a radical life for Christ. Be a radical worshiper who is sold out for the kingdom of God and not for your own agenda or motives.

God's people, the company of worshipers who are sold out to Jesus Christ, are called to be leaders on the earth. Be radical in your service to God and in your expression of love and devotion to Him. If you are radical, people around you will want to be radical too. It just takes one excellent worshiper to break rank to give everyone else permission to do the same. Be the one to break rank and reach for the excellence of God's presence. Don't wait for someone else; *you* lead the pursuit for God.

I never want to get to the place where our worship team is simply "great at what we do." That would be awful. Radical effort is required if we want His name to be lifted magnificently, throughout every sphere of influence possible. We can't lift His name by trying to be "cool." I often have the opportunity to travel and speak to church music teams. Many worship teams are working hard to get their craft together. They are trying to get a bigger choir and a better sound system. They're wishing they had better musicians, they wonder if the choir should wear colored vests, and they try to get everything just right. These are all wonderful goals, and I *love* bringing excellence to the house of God, but I encourage teams to check their motivation. Don't fall into the trap of worshiping the worship. Worship the King and bring excellence because you love Him.

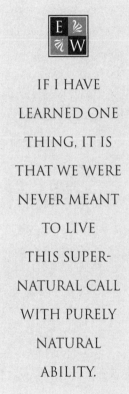

IF I HAVE LEARNED ONE THING, IT IS THAT WE WERE NEVER MEANT TO LIVE THIS SUPER-NATURAL CALL WITH PURELY NATURAL ABILITY.

We have a most divine promise that when God is lifted up, He draws all men unto His glorious self. Psalm 91:1 says, "He who dwells in the shelter of the Most High will rest in the shadow of the Almighty." If you feel like you are continually running on empty, then you need to respond to His instruction, obey the Spirit of God, and *get in His presence*. Joy and strength are found in His dwelling place, in His presence. If I have learned one thing, it is that we were never meant to live this supernatural call with purely natural ability. We will never make it on our own strength. But if we take God at His Word, live in His presence, live a life of love, and respond to His voice, then we will live our entire lifetime growing in the knowledge of Christ, remaining fresh and strong in the Word, and living a life that people will want to follow.

There is a beautiful song called "With All My Heart," written by Babbie Mason. Every time I hear this song, I am reminded of why I do what I am doing.

This is such a beautiful song. I often take this CD with me on a plane and have been blown away many times by the simple but powerful lyrics. We can be talented and gifted, but in the end Babbie's song must be our heart's cry, because all the talent in the world isn't enough. Excellent worship is not merely singing a song or playing music in the sanctuary. To step into all that God is asking us to step into at this time, we must be dedicated disciples who are living surrendered lives away from the sanctuary. What we say as we walk into any room needs to reflect a heart of worship for God.

This simple truth is powerful—*All that we do for Him and gain because of Him is all futile, unless we are deeply planted in Him.*

Acts 17:28 says, "For in him we live and move and have our being." So we keep our hearts on course by truly loving and seeking Him above all else. "But blessed is the man who trusts in the Lord, *whose confidence is in him*" (Jeremiah 17:7, emphasis added).

A TRANSPARENT HEART

Jeremiah 17:9 warns us, "The heart is deceitful above all things." We're instructed to trust in the Lord with all of our heart and not to lean on our own understanding. We're to acknowledge the Lord in all our ways, and He will direct our path. I challenge you to develop tenacious

WITH ALL MY HEART

IN THIS QUIET PLACE WITH YOU
I BOW BEFORE YOUR THRONE
I BARE THE DEEPEST PART OF ME
TO YOU AND YOU ALONE
I KEEP NO SECRETS, FOR THERE IS NO THOUGHT
YOU HAVE NOT KNOWN
I BRING MY BEST AND ALL THE REST
TO YOU AND LAY THEM DOWN
WITH ALL MY HEART I WANT TO LOVE YOU, LORD
AND LIVE MY LIFE EACH DAY TO KNOW YOU MORE
ALL THAT IS IN ME IS YOURS COMPLETELY
I WILL SERVE YOU ONLY WITH ALL MY HEART
YOU FAITHFULLY SUPPLY MY NEEDS
ACCORDING TO YOUR PLAN
SO HELP ME, LORD, TO SEEK YOUR FACE
BEFORE I SEEK YOUR HAND
AND TRUST YOU KNOW WHAT'S BEST FOR ME
WHEN I DON'T UNDERSTAND
THEN FOLLOW IN OBEDIENCE
IN EVERY CIRCUMSTANCE

trust in God. Some worshipers find it easier to open their hearts and express genuine love and devotion to the Lord than others. Sometimes past hurts, regrets, disappointments, or simply a fear of being let down prevents a heart from being completely transparent.

**WHEN WE ARE IN THE PRESENCE OF THE LORD,
WE BECOME TRANSPARENT AND HONEST,
AND OUR HEARTS AND SOULS CRY OUT FOR HIM.**

When we are in the presence of the Lord, we become transparent and honest, and our hearts and souls cry out for Him. Psalm 51:10–13 says well what the prayer of our hearts should be: "Create in me a pure heart, O God, and renew a steadfast spirit within me. Do not cast me from your presence or take your Holy Spirit from me. Restore to me the joy of your salvation and grant me a willing spirit, to sustain me. Then I will teach transgressors your ways, and sinners will turn back to you." *The Message* Bible puts it in everyday language:

> *Soak me in your laundry and I'll come out clean, scrub me and I'll have a snow-white life. Tune me in to foot-tapping songs, set these once-broken bones to dancing. Don't look too close for blemishes, give me a clean bill of health. God, make a fresh start in me, shape a Genesis week from the chaos of my life. Don't throw me out with the trash, or fail to breathe holiness in me. Bring me back from gray exile, put a fresh wind in my sails! Give me a job teaching rebels your ways so the lost can find their way home.* (THE MESSAGE)

When Isaiah caught sight of God, he was moved to confess his sin (Isaiah 6). When our humanness is confronted by the magnificence and holiness of God, we become very aware of our need for God's grace and His cleansing power in our lives. If we have unforgiveness, anger, jealousy, or bitterness, we only need to ask God to forgive us, and He will powerfully remove it from our hearts. Romans 12:1 teaches us how to live this life of worship and love: "Therefore, I urge you, brothers, in

WHEN YOU WORSHIP HIM,

THE MASK IS REMOVED

AND THE TRUTH

IS REVEALED . . . IT IS

PRESENTED TO THE FATHER . . .

HIS PRESENCE INVADES

YOUR SITUATION

AND HE KISSES AWAY

YOUR TEARS

view of God's mercy, to offer your bodies as living sacrifices, holy and pleasing to God—this is your spiritual act of worship." As we worship God, the Holy Spirit gently exposes what is in our hearts. He will peel back all of the unclean layers, all the protective barriers we have placed there, and make our hearts clean and pure again. It is amazing to see that happen in worship!

You may not want the layers of your heart to be exposed; maybe that's a scary thought for you. But God is a faithful and loving God, and He wants to peel off any callused layers on your heart so that you can be restored. He will not humiliate you or hurt you, but He longs for you to be restored to a place of wholeness in Him. From that place of wholeness, you can be all that He has planned for you to become. So pursue with passion the presence of God and let Him, rather than the people around you, work on your heart.

"He will have no fear of bad news; his heart is steadfast, trusting in the Lord. His heart is secure, he will have no fear; in the end he will look in triumph on his foes" (Psalm 112:7–8).

Jesus laid the foundation of *life* before us when He said, "Love the Lord your God with all your heart and with all your soul and with all your mind. This is the first and greatest commandment" (Matthew 22:37–38).

The song of the heart that loves the Lord is the song that will resound in heaven.

Chapter Eight

EXPECT THE UNEXPECTED

EXPECT THE UNEXPECTED

One day as he [Jesus] was teaching, Pharisees and teachers of the
law, who had come from every village of Galilee and from Judea and
Jerusalem, were sitting there. And the power of the Lord was present
for him to heal the sick. Some men came carrying a paralytic on a mat
and tried to take him into the house to lay him before Jesus. When they
could not find a way to do this because of the crowd, they went up on
the roof and lowered him on his mat through the tiles into the
middle of the crowd, right in front of Jesus.
(Luke 5:17–19)

I love this story of radical faith in action! I can imagine the conversation of these compassionate friends as they stood outside of the crowded
building that housed the presence of the Savior.

"What shall we do to get our friend to Jesus?" asks one friend of the
sick man to the other.

Then a smile spreads across the face of his companion as he answers,
"Whatever it takes!"

Unified in purpose, teamed with determination, they push through
the crowd and scale the side of the house while shifting the weight of
their friend on their backs. "Whatever it takes!" the other agrees as they
break through the roof. These excellent worshipers lowered their friend
down through the ceiling and into the lap of Jesus. And when Jesus
saw the faith of these radical believers, he said, "Friend, your sins are
forgiven."

FAITH AND EXPECTATION

The first thing you can bring to worship is your radical faith and expectation. Jesus loves it when you bring faith into the sanctuary. Jesus healed the sick man because of the faith of his friends. Don't we all hope to have excellent friends like these when we need faith for a miracle?

What sort of faith, what sort of expectation, do you carry into the sanctuary? Your faith could bring a miracle for someone else. If you want to be an excellent worshiper, ask yourself, "What am I contributing toward the service?" Am I eager to get to church on Sunday morning? Am I packing my friends into the car who need to see Jesus? Or am I moaning all the way to church, late for choir rehearsal, and scowling upon arrival from a stinking attitude? Do I dawdle in, hoping someone else has already prayed in the presence of God?

If you bring to the altar a lack of faith, if you expect nothing, you will most likely have your expectation fulfilled. But if you bring your faith, first and foremost, *Jesus moves.*

When I think about what Jesus Christ has done in my life, I am filled with expectation of miracles for others. When I think of the way I felt before I found Jesus, and what I thought I was destined for, and what Jesus saved me from, and what He has put inside me, and where He has placed me now; when I think on these things, faith rises and explodes within me. I become eager to get to church and see His presence fill the sanctuary as we worship Him.

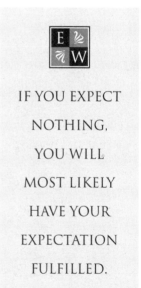

IF YOU EXPECT NOTHING, YOU WILL MOST LIKELY HAVE YOUR EXPECTATION FULFILLED.

Some people may fear that others will judge them when they publicly worship God. They may worry that someone will criticize their radical display of affection to the Lord and disclose them as superficial or shallow. But don't let what others think rob you of enjoying the supernatural presence of God that comes when we worship Him from the depths of our hearts. True worship is not about stirring ourselves into an emotional frenzy. Jesus Christ is real, and what He has done in our lives is worthy of our extravagant praise. What He has done is worthy of our getting up at any hour of the morning to worship Him. If we will worship Him as He deserves, we will be full of faith, full of the glory of the Lord, and full of His presence.

When I lead worship, I think of the people who sit in the congregation. Some have been on shift work all week. Some haven't spent a second with the Lord since last Sunday's service. Some have been up with the kids all night. Some are just plain faithful people. It excites me to realize that corporate worship in the church will help to turn their eyes to the Lord. It thrills me to know that our time of worship together will take them from their situation and point them toward the Lord. Our worship team never wants to direct people toward us—we simply want to do whatever it takes to lead people into the presence of Jesus.

TRUE WORSHIP IS NOT ABOUT STIRRING OURSELVES INTO AN EMOTIONAL FRENZY.

Don't be hesitant to bring visible faith and exuberant expectations into your time of worship. It is not shallow; it is awesome. I love that Jesus was pleased when the guys dropped their friend through the roof to Him. I can imagine Him saying, "Cool; I love your faith. I *see* your faith; I am moved by your faith, so here you go—be healed."

JOY

Our pastor, Brian Houston, often talks about the "zombie spirit" in the sanctuary. You know, that dull, glazed-over look in people's eyes that comes when they forget what God has done for them and where He is leading them. We need to bring joy into our time of worship. If visitors can't see any difference between our church and the club down the road, then we have a problem. Or if the club down the road is actually better at bringing joy to people, then we have an even bigger problem!

When you walk into church on Sunday morning, do you feel the impact of joy inside of you? The joy of the Lord is your strength, and what Jesus has done in your life should put the largest smile on your face. True worship fills you with joy despite what circumstances are going on around us. No matter what you are facing, all circumstances must bow to the Word of the Lord, and that truth alone should put joy on your face.

The Word says, "You are the light of the world. A city that is set on a hill cannot be hidden. Nor do they light a lamp and put it under a basket, but on a lampstand, and it gives light to all who are in the house. Let your light so shine before men, that they may see your good works and glorify your Father in heaven" (Matthew 5:14–16 KJV). Sometimes I suggest to our worship teams that they stand in front of the mirror and practice joy. Some people *think* they look joyful but when they see themselves on a video they realize they are "hiding the light" of their true feelings for God.

> IT DOESN'T WORK TO HAVE A TEAM OF PEOPLE LEADING WORSHIP IF THEY LOOK ZONED OUT.

Let the joy of the Lord show on your face. When Moses came down from Mount Sinai with the Ten Commandments in his hands, "he was not aware that his face was radiant because he had spoken with the Lord" (Exodus 34:29). I love that spending time with Jesus literally shows on your face! When the reality of Jesus Christ setting you free is inside you, it will show on your face. Don't be afraid to let the glory of the Lord shine through your life.

When we audition people for our choir, it's true that they must be able to sing, but the second thing we look for is that the individual is able to show the joy of the Lord through his or her countenance. It doesn't work to have a team of people leading worship if they look zoned out. When you have people who are radical for Christ, and their joy is visible, it makes a difference in the church. It's the same for everyone. Often the musicians and the guys who stand farther back on the platform think it doesn't matter if the joy of the Lord is on their face, but it does. It only takes one person on the platform looking like a zombie to become a distraction to everyone.

Imagine if an unbelieving visitor came to a church where the joy of the Lord was visible on every face both on the platform and in the pews. Imagine the revival that would hit that church. You have the ability to change the atmosphere of your sanctuary by bringing liberating joy into your worship. Joy is a natural result of spending time in the presence of the Lord.

EXTREMES ACTUALLY DRAW MORE ATTENTION TO THE WORSHIPERS THAN TO THE ONE WHO IS TO BE WORSHIPED.

EBB AND FLOW ON THE PLATFORM

I have found there is a natural ebb and flow to worship. There is enthusiastic high praise, and then there is deep, rich worship. But there is always joy and an overwhelming expectation. There are extremes in some styles of corporate worship that can alienate people from participating in worship that is spiritual and truthful. When I encourage people to abandon their reserves and worship the Lord, I want to balance that exhortation with caution that worship will still be orderly and directed by the Holy Spirit, who is not the author of confusion.

Our team is careful of being too reflective or too overwhelmingly loud, because we want to "draw all men" to the Lord. We don't want to draw attention to ourselves or to alienate anyone from the gospel because of showmanship in the sanctuary.

SOVEREIGN
VISITATIONS
FROM THE
LORD DO
HAPPEN, BUT
DON'T TRY
TO MANU-
FACTURE
THEM.

So we have the two extremes to contend with: the "zombie spirit" and what I call "sweating blood." I've gone into some services where the worship team has exploded with praise, and half an hour later they are still at it full speed. No one has taken a breath, and it looks as if veins are about to break and blood might pour through the sweat on people's faces. When people in the church look like they're in shock, the worship is no longer spiritual! Such aerobics will most certainly alienate people. Then the other extreme is when people go into that reflective, melancholy kind of worship and forget they're not alone in the room. When people look like they are lower than worms, their worship is no longer truthful.

These extremes actually draw more attention to the worshipers than to the One who is to be worshiped. When the Holy Spirit leads people in worship, there is a natural ebb and flow to the times of high praise and deep worship that builds up the spirits of those who participate.

If you have the privilege of leading worship, be considerate of the time. "Free worship" doesn't need to go on for two hours. How awesome a service is and how long it lasts are totally irrelevant. Sovereign visitations from the Lord do happen, but don't try to manufacture them. It does not help to build the church if the worship team is having a great time and totally misses the fact that everyone else in the church has fallen asleep or left for a cup of coffee!

At Hillsong Church, we have extreme moments of praise, and then we will often pull it back so that people can hear the voice of God speak to them in the stillness of His presence. Sometimes worshipers run right over what God is trying to say to them! But with that ebb and flow of worship, we are aiming to keep everyone together, because we want to see *everyone* engage in bringing their worship before the King. In corporate worship we need to open our ears spiritually and musically in order to lead the multitudes in a genuine expression of love and adoration of our Savior.

KNOW WHAT YOUR PASTOR EXPECTS

The more you love to worship the Lord, the more likely it will be that you may become part of a worship team, or if your church service is televised, you may be viewed by the world as a team worshiper. Though this chapter is mostly directed to those who lead worship teams, I trust that individual worshipers will grasp knowledge from the pages that will enhance the sincerity of their worship.

To those who lead or serve on worship teams: I advise you to find out what your pastor expects from you. For an individual worshiper who wants to support the move of the Spirit from your place in the sanctuary, this section will illustrate to you some of the technicalities that are needed to keep order in the service so you will know why it's important to follow your pastor's lead. I thank God we work with a pastor who knows what he wants from our worship team. He expects us to be full of faith for the service and to bring excellence to the sanctuary.

The hardest thing I encounter when visiting other churches is that the music leaders don't always know what their pastor wants from the worship time. I'm referring here to details such as whether or not to sing during altar calls and offerings. Altar calls are divine moments, and yet if a microphone is going to give feedback or if a baby is going to cry, it seems to happen at the most sensitive times of worship. A worship team must know how to support the pastor throughout the entire service.

Worshipers can't relax or sit down and dream through the altar call; this is a time when we must pray to God. The musicians might start to play, and then as the pastor indicates for us to sing, we are to be ready to build faith in that meeting through our praise. Worshipers on the platform and in the sanctuary are called to pray and be ready to support the pastor as he leads the church service.

Support your pastor. When he calls the church to worship, bring faith and sensitivity to the Holy Spirit. Undergird what the pastor is doing and help him to bring in the net. We cast out the spiritual nets with our songs of praise, and then we stand in awe as God draws all men unto himself. Music that expresses what is happening spiritually has a powerful dynamic attached to it: it is then being used for its designed purpose.

Our offering is an important part of worship, and again, we are to bring our faith to this part of the service. It isn't a time to wave at our friends in the fourth row. It isn't a time for the musicians to practice that weird bridge on an upcoming song! Worshipers are to stand strong, full of faith and attention, to support what the pastor is saying and doing. Keep your heart ready to worship and know what your pastor expects; if you don't know, *ask* him!

LEARN HOW TO LISTEN, LOOK, AND BE AWARE

Worship God with everything you are, but have "one eye shut and one eye open." It's so easy to get lost in worship, and while that is awesome for you, you could easily miss a great moment. Be aware of what is happening corporately in the service, whether you are on the platform or sitting in the congregation. The worship leaders have the responsibility of taking people into the presence of the Lord as a team *together*. Things like key changes and stops of songs are vital. Musically, if a "train crash" occurs, often it happens because someone on the platform wasn't looking, listening, or staying alert. When we don't stay alert to what's going on around us in our personal life, we can get ourselves into trouble. I found this out one day when I received a phone call at my church office letting me know the police were looking for me at my house. At the gas service station that morning, I had been on the phone, lost in a quite intense conversation, which had been going on for a long time. Apparently I even filled up the tank while I was on the phone (and that's really dangerous!) and then left without paying! The police told me all this because they had watched me on the video! I hadn't paid for the gasoline I put in my car that morning! I was now a worship pastor *and* a criminal! I'd never done that before in my life!

So the police were at my house, and Melinda (who is amazing and helps me with the children) had the grand delight of welcoming the police into the house. I then had to explain to them that I wasn't a thief. I was just so engrossed in what I was doing that it didn't even occur to me that I hadn't paid. I didn't even think about it; I just hopped into the car and drove off to church—how embarrassing!

Likewise, we can be so engrossed in loving Jesus during the worship time that we forget our responsibilities to those around us. It's wonderful to enjoy what we are doing, but when half the band changes key and the other half doesn't, then the entire congregation slides to a halt, while the musicians head for the chorus and the singers are back at verse one. When this happens, our eyes come off of Jesus.

GREAT PRODUCTION
SOUND AND LIGHTING

Human beings are amazing creatures who seem to need everything "just right" in order to have an excellent church service. As leaders we know that a substandard production makes for an awful service! When sound is too loud, it is a distraction. When sound is too soft, it is a distraction. When sound is feeding back, it is a distraction. When the lighting is dark, it makes people sleepy. If we create a bedroom setting, people will sit down and just nod off during the preaching! If the air-conditioning is too warm, people get sleepy, and too cold makes them cranky. Things like this detract from having an excellent worship service.

If the preacher's lapel microphone isn't working, it detracts. It stops momentum. It stops the flow of the service. People take their eyes off Jesus. So it is critical that we work toward getting all the elements right. Production people are as critical a part of the worship team as the worship leader. Without them, nothing is seen or heard. One thing I love about our Hillsong production team is that they are filled with enthusiasm. Enthusiasm stems from a strong belief in something—something convincing. That belief and conviction bring power—a burning desire to put our thoughts and beliefs into action.

It's easy to walk in the middle of the road and be average. Whenever someone dares to break rank and become enthusiastic about something, there'll always be someone who thinks they are being unrealistic or obsessive. But who cares? The truth is, people who are obsessed or unrealistic about an idea get more done than people who are without enthusiasm. Colossians 3:23 says, "Whatever you do, work at it with all your heart, as working for the Lord, not for men." Dave Watson, the production manager of Hillsong Church, has brought such enthusiasm to the team that it has increased in numbers, and he has broken the mold of what a godly production team is.

As an excellent worshiper, I encourage you to keep your eyes on Jesus, even when all the technicalities of sound and lights fail. Don't let distractions keep you from seeing the beauty of the Lord. Your enthusiasm will minister to the worship team as they work to get back on the track of excellence.

PASSION

Are you passionate about Jesus Christ? I look at my Bible in the morning, and I start to cry. It holds every answer to life that you will ever need. I look at it, and it holds it all there for me. I am constantly reminded of what God did to save us and to set us free. Allow yourself to think about the Lord and what *He has done*. Allow passion for the Lord to rise within you; let passion be the fuel that drives who you are and what you do in life.

Every time I get off track and start to run under my own steam, it's always because I've taken my eyes off Jesus and let my passion for Him start to wane. Passion for the Lord is not found on a platform. To be beautifully passionate about the truth of God's Word, you must really *know* Him.

What can kill your passion? Think about it in the context of marriage. What are some of the passion killers of relationships? Lack of interest, indifference, and being too busy to take time to be together destroys passion. It's a huge passion killer if one partner is saying, "Oh, my sweet, I love you," but the other is off in her own little world somewhere and not listening. Distraction is a passion killer.

Mark and I have a rule that when we walk into our bedroom, we don't talk about work, because we honor the intimacy of our relationship. Jumping into bed while whining about work and other current events, and then trying to get passionate . . . guess what, there is nothing there for each other. Our passion left the room when the whining began. Can you see what I'm saying?

Spend intimate time with the Lord. Don't be too busy and don't go to Him complaining, giving your top-ten list of wants and then say, "Amen." Go to Him, thank Him, love Him, and allow Him to love you in return.

DON'T TALK TOO MUCH

When asked, I always tell worship leaders, "Don't talk too much." Too much of anything great takes the greatness of it away. We *lead* worship by being the first to worship. The pastor will preach the message. If he ever asks us to preach, that will be a great honor and a privilege—and we would do an awesome job—but until that invitation comes, we must stick to leading the worship and doing what we have been asked to do. Be committed to the entire service and not merely your role. If you are only committed to your own responsibilities, and you forget about everything else, then what are you really contributing?

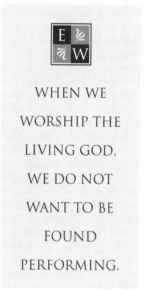

WHEN WE WORSHIP THE LIVING GOD, WE DO NOT WANT TO BE FOUND PERFORMING.

BE GENUINE

Excellent worshipers are genuine. That performance mentality must submit to serve the body of Christ. When we worship the living God, we do not want to be found performing. We need to be genuine in our purpose of worship.

The world can tell when someone is pretending. Be an excellent worshiper whose pursuit of God is genuine in commitment. Then if people do see you while you're worshiping the Lord, they will fall in love with Jesus all over again.

NO PRIMA DONNAS

At Hillsong Conference, we did a hilarious skit to illustrate the sad picture of worshipers who want the attention to be on them. The skit begins with the group of faithful production people and a few singers and musicians on stage. They arrive early to the platform to rehearse and to prepare the stage, etc., and then after the service starts, in walks the worship leader looking for his microphone, whining about the feedback of the speakers, and demanding a glass of water! It was funny, and a little scary, because when I asked the conferees if this was anything like their "real life" experience, too many people put up their hands!

The "prima donna" attitude is so subtle. It whispers to the unguarded heart of the worshiper, *Man, this church wouldn't be as good if I wasn't here. If only the church knew what they had in my being here. All the pastors get paid—they should pay me for all I do! Don't they know how much I'm worth?*

The prima donna, "look at me, look at me" attitude does not glorify God. People are promoted because of their faithfulness and the call of God on their life. The excellent worshipers never seek promotions, but honor is graced upon them from the Lord.

Worship is sovereign. The story in Luke 14:17–21 tells of a man who sent his servant out to tell those who had been invited to the banquet: "Come, everything is now ready."

But they all began to make excuses.

The first said, "I have just bought a field, and I must go and see it. Please excuse me."

Another said, "I have just bought five yoke of oxen, and I'm on my way to try them out. Please excuse me."

Still another said, "I have just gotten married, so I can't come."

The servant came back and reported this to his master. Then the owner of the house became angry and ordered his servant, "Go out quickly into the streets and alleys of the town and bring in the poor, the crippled, the blind, and the lame."

The people that were too busy to attend the banquet could be any one of us. But we can also be one of the people who drop everything in order to come to the banquet of the Lord and say, "Yes, I'll have a go. I love Jesus, I've got this bit of talent; it needs a bit of work, but I've got it and I'll work on it. Yes, I'll have a go at it!" Jesus grabs ordinary people, people committed to Him, committed to His plan and His purpose, and He uses them.

When I travel I meet people who seem desperate for recognition. Don't feel like you are going to miss out. Be faithful, follow after the things of God; be genuine, be passionate in your pursuit, and *trust* God.

"The race is not to the swift or the battle to the strong, nor does food come to the wise or wealth to the brilliant or favor to the learned; but time and chance happen to them all" (Ecclesiastes 9:11).

Walk away from the prima donna attitude. Walk away from doing things in the church for recognition, and be committed to building the church—God's lighthouse to the world. God will answer the needs in the earth today through people like you and me. Just the ordinary, everyday guys, who say, "Excuse me, but I would like to do something for the Lord. If you can possibly use me, feel free!"

Jesus said, "Whoever wants to become great among you must be your servant, and whoever wants to be first must be your slave—just as the Son of Man did not come to be served, but to serve, and to give his life as a ransom for many" (Matthew 20:26–28). God honors servants, not prima donnas!

ERICA'S STORY

This story belongs to Erica Crocker, one of my great friends, who is a tremendous singer and an asset to our team. Here's her story on walking down the "prima donna" road:

Basically, when I came to the church, I joined the choir, and a couple of weeks after I joined I asked if I could be a front singer. I come from a show business family (I think I had the "spirit of show business" on me). It actually took three and a half years before I became a front singer, because God had to do a work in me.

All those "enemies of the platform" Darlene has talked about . . . I was doing, and He had to work through each one of them! So I was in the choir, and my dad used to say to me, "If you can see the camera, the camera can see you." So the camera used to pan across the front, and I used to make sure I was in the front line of the choir. I would be singing quite normally, but if I could see the camera coming, I would really be "worshiping God." Well . . . with one eye anyway. The other one was focused on the video monitor, making sure I looked good!

Then, all of a sudden, one day the choir leader discovered that I was too tall to be in the front row because there were people behind me who were shorter, and so she sent me up into the back row of the choir. I hated that, because . . . hey, the camera can't see you if you're at the back of the choir! So I used to get there early and I would stand in the front and I would crouch down a bit to make myself shorter. I would get away with it in rehearsal, but once we started, I would get sore knees, and then it was, "Hey, Crocker . . . get up in the back!"

So I ended up at the back a lot. Even when I was at the back, though, I was always trying to get on the corner so that I could still be seen. . . .

ANYWAY . . . one day I was up in the back (I wasn't on the end, so the camera couldn't see me), and I had a real attitude going on toward the lady who was directing the choir. So I was standing in the back behind someone so I couldn't see her, and she couldn't see me.

So there I was "worshiping God" (HA!), and the worship leader was reading a verse out of the Bible about tongues of fire, and we had these pyrotechnics go off, and I was just like "Wow" . . . and God opened my ears. We started singing this song, and as I was singing it the music was so incredible. I was surrounded by singers singing sincerely to God. I'm sure it had always been like that, but I had never heard it before. All of a sudden my ears were opened (maybe I had a blockage, and the explosion set it free), and I was standing there, and God spoke to me in my spirit, and He said, "Why are you here?" So I answered Him and said, "What do you mean? I am here singing, singing in this choir." Then He said to me, "No, that's not what it's about. You are here to worship me, and we are going to be worshiping here forever and ever and ever. And the whole idea is that the people out there are worshiping; not looking at you, they are looking at me. No matter where you are, whether you are on the platform, out front being a backup singer, in the car park, or in the congregation, you are there to worship me." From that day on, my life changed. Our Wednesday night rehearsals no longer became an option. I was there for everything, always "Yes sir, yes ma'am, I'm there, whatever." So that's my story.

Erica is the best. I think she is so gutsy to be that honest, because we have all been there! God changed that spirit that wanted everyone to "look at me, look at me" so that she could worship Him extravagantly and excellently in spirit and in truth. Awesome! *I love you,* Erica Crocker, and am so glad God put us together.

LOVE THE LORD MORE THAN YOUR GIFT

Loving the Lord more than your gift keeps worship in perspective. We become frustrated when we become very self-reflective, looking on our gift and wondering why it isn't being used in the way we want it to. Then we get together with other people who are feeling the same way, and we share our frustrations and start walking down the bitterness road.

Misery, gossip, and bitterness will always find a friend. The fact that we can find someone to agree with us is *not* confirmation from the Lord that what we're feeling is right! No matter what we whine about, we will always find someone with the same attitude who is happy to agree with

us because it makes them feel better! That is actually a dangerous path to follow.

Discipline yourself to keep your focus on the Lord. If God wants to birth incredible things in you, there is no man that can stand in the way of what He wants to do. God is your promoter.

"No one from the east or the west or from the desert can exalt a man. But it is God who judges: He brings one down, he exalts another" (Psalm 75:6–7).

Be faithful with what He has put in your hand, because in the end, it is all about Jesus.

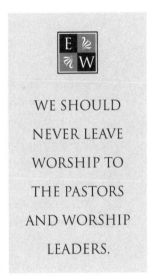

WE SHOULD NEVER LEAVE WORSHIP TO THE PASTORS AND WORSHIP LEADERS.

PRACTICAL TIPS FOR EXCELLENT WORSHIPERS

I found this piece of correspondence that I sent to all of our Hillsong Church worship leaders and music directors. This is word for word as I gave it to them, and it may give you more insight into some of the expectations we have of our team, but its principles apply to all those who long to be excellent worshipers of Jesus:

Dearest Worship Leaders and Music Directors,
As each new day unfolds, I'm so critically aware of the power of praising and worshiping our dearest Lord Jesus.
The spiritual temperature continues to rise and the battle

*between heaven and hell for the lives of precious people is ON!
So . . .*

Spiritually . . .

*Stay close to God . . . when you are in His presence, you
become so aware that "Greater is He that is in me, than he that is
in the world!" that the striving ceases . . . you begin to relax and
allow who you are in Christ to SHINE!*

*Increase your dedication to prayer and holding up the service
continually to the Lord in prayer. Be unceasing in your prayer.*

*Understand that you cannot be led by "feelings," as often we
may "feel" the service was FLAT, etc., but the Holy Spirit is moving
in people's hearts and lives. Lead from a position of FAITH, an
unswerving commitment to the unseen.*

Leadership . . .

*Whoever is leading worship is the person who is given the
authority to LEAD in the direction they feel. They are directly
answerable to myself and Pastor Brian.*

*The music director wholeheartedly supports the worship leader
in any decision the worship leader makes . . . whether it is their
personal opinion or not.*

*I believe that UNITY (a commitment to oneness, which contin-
ually takes a dying to self, YIELDING, all the HARD things!) will
cause great DAMAGE in the enemy's camp and bring increased
effectiveness in the Kingdom of God. In Psalm 133, the anointing
oil, described as a result of unity, is also deemed "COSTLY" . . . it
personally costs a lot. Stay committed to it!*

*Lead by example, be supportive in the service, love your team,
be PUNCTUAL, be PREPARED musically, be ready for anything! The
more preparation you commit to the rehearsal, the more room
you'll have to step out in the prophetic, to play the unexpected, to
release the "MOMENTS" in church life that make a service special.*

REMEMBER,

You are a part of a champion team.

You belong to a church family who is committed to seeing your destiny unfold.

You are greatly appreciated and loved, not just for what you bring to this house . . . but for WHO YOU ARE IN CHRIST!

Have an outstanding night and pray for "mixdown" that the Spirit of God makes Himself at home in this project (album).

I love you dearly,

Darlene

WHAT YOU BRING TO
THE WORSHIP SERVICE

Worship is a divine privilege, and with that privilege comes a great responsibility to show generosity to others in the body of Christ through all we do. We should never leave worship to the pastors and worship leaders. We all need to learn to be excellent, extravagant worshipers, generous in our service to one another and generous in our expression of love toward one another—it will change the dynamics of this harvest.

Chapter Nine

EVERLASTING
MUSIC

EVERLASTING MUSIC

From the beginning of time God has been worshiped with music and praise. Even as God laid the earth's foundation, "the morning stars sang together and all the angels shouted for joy" (Job 38:4–7). The first account we have of God's people praising Him with music is when Moses and the Israelites sang an incredible hymn of praise, thanking God for His spectacular win over Pharaoh and his army. Their shouts of joy must have sounded so victorious as they sang, "The Lord is my strength and my song; he has become my salvation. He is my God, and I will praise him, my father's God, and I will exalt him" (Exodus 15:1–7). Singing was the immediate response of the children of Israel to God's incredible deliverance. Notice they never sang to each other, but they responded to the Lord with a song of praise to Him.

Music is a powerful force, created by God to stir the core of a person like nothing else can. I am so thankful to have been surrounded by the beautiful sound of music my entire life. From the day I was born and every day since, music has had an incredible pull on my life. I have sung so many melodies. My parents both sang, and my brothers and sister all sing. I have danced since I can remember; I learned jazz, tap, and ballet for nine years; and I have studied piano and voice from five years of age until now. When I was young, I wrote many simple tunes, and I dreamed of one day presenting these musical ideas to someone other than myself. I had many dreams, yet none of them made sense until I finally met Jesus, my dream maker. In meeting Him, I finally understood the reason I had this dream. The more I know Him, the more I understand the power of the music that is so real inside me.

The first worship song I ever wrote was after I was saved at the age of fifteen. Our church sang it one night, and rather than feeling elated to hear my song being sung, the spiritual responsibility of putting a praise and worship song in someone else's heart overwhelmed me. For the next five years I wrote soppy love songs instead! I didn't write another worship song until I understood more about the power of worshiping God "in spirit and in truth."

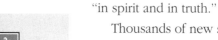

MUSIC IS A POWERFUL FORCE, CREATED BY GOD TO STIR THE CORE OF A PERSON LIKE NOTHING ELSE CAN.

Thousands of new songs are written about our King every day, which is incredible! Sometimes I feel like they all land in the form of demo tapes on my desk! Some are eagerly sent from awesome musicians from around the world asking for direction and an opinion, others are from our Hillsong writers who are edging their ear toward heaven and desiring to bring a fresh sound to the earth. Some are musical masterpieces and some are incredibly simple in the form they take, but I am continually amazed by the seemingly endless ideas and countless soul-stirring melodies and lyrics that are composed by writers who try to describe the wonder of our King.

I don't claim to be the greatest and most knowledgeable when it comes to the craft of songwriting, but I do have an ear for the songs that give the church a new message to sing. The church always embraces new melodies that allow worshipers to express the song in their hearts to our Lord and King. Every now and again God breathes His anointing on a song, and it finds its way into the mouths, minds, and hearts of congregations all over the world.

Twenty-first-century hymns and anthems are being written and sung by crowds that defy age barriers. These songs are made accessible to be sung by even the least musical person, and they ignite passion and fire inside everyone that enters into its expression of praise. Songwriters such as Matt Redman, Martin Smith, and Reuben Morgan, to list a few, have the ability to write songs that cause the human spirit to react in a powerful way. Their songs don't allow us to remain the same.

The Lord is sending new songs for us to sing. They are prophetic songs. They are songs of praise. They are songs of unity, songs of intimacy, and songs of war. They are rising among us, restoring peace and righteousness. They are songs of grace and forgiveness, songs of mercy and compassion, songs of strength and justice, and songs of power and might. The sound of worship is being restored to its rightful place and being offered to its only Benefactor.

As we embrace these new songs, let's also remember the great anthems written over the centuries by legends such as Charles Wesley, who wrote approximately sixty-five hundred hymns. Charles was a phenomenal writer and penned awe-inspiring songs such as "Hark! the Herald Angels Sing" and "O for a Thousand Tongues to Sing."

A songwriter could go to a hundred classes on how to create great songs or how to write "hit" songs, but the craft is only a part of the writer's commission when it comes to bringing the sound of heaven to earth. One doesn't accidentally write a heaven song. Songs that truly connect the spirit of man with his Creator will always be birthed through the well-worn path to the throne room of God, a path the writer has traveled to and from many times.

I pray that we bring the sound of heaven to earth, that we let "His

SONGS THAT TRULY CONNECT THE SPIRIT OF MAN WITH HIS CREATOR WILL ALWAYS BE BIRTHED THROUGH THE WELL-WORN PATH TO THE THRONE ROOM OF GOD.

will be done and His kingdom come on earth as it is in heaven." We don't need to wait for the world to create a new sound for us to copy as best we can. I have heard some remarkably godly songs on the secular radio lately, and I know that most of the writers don't even know what they have tapped into. These songs from unsaved writers that touch the heart of God are examples of "the stones crying out" (Luke 19:40) to worship Him. We must not let the stones of the earth praise God more than we who know Him.

The Word says, "Creation waits in eager expectation for the sons of God to be revealed" (Romans 8:19). More songs must be birthed out of the full knowledge that we, God's own sons and daughters, have of Him. God is to be praised! We must take our rightful places in this chorus of praise so that the glory of the Lord will be seen through all the earth. A Christian musician intuitively knows the difference between simply playing music and playing music that touches God's heart. A songwriter in the kingdom must have a heart that pursues the things of God and *not* the praises of men.

Mark and I were invited to attend a songwriters' dinner in the United States, where writers whom I had long admired gathered together to honor Christian songwriters of the century, Bill and Gloria Gaither. Amy Grant, her husband, Vince, and Michael W. Smith presented a powerful medley of some of the Gaithers' much-loved songs. Mark and I were ministered to as they sang song after song, such as "Because He Lives, I Can Face Tomorrow," "Jesus, Jesus, There Is Just Something About That Name," "Something Beautiful," and "The King Is Coming."

> A CHRISTIAN MUSICIAN INTUITIVELY KNOWS THE DIFFERENCE BETWEEN SIMPLY PLAYING MUSIC AND PLAYING MUSIC THAT TOUCHES GOD'S HEART.

I thank God for this godly couple, who wrote the music and praise songs that were like a soundtrack to my own salvation story. Needless to say, Mark and I wept as we were reminded of God's greatness in our lives—and how much we have to thank Him for.

At Hillsong, even with all the recording projects we do and new songs we bring to record, I always encourage our writers to never become project-based writers. We must always be heaven-based writers whose hearts are desperate to catch the "new song" in everything we write. A passion for our songs to be pure in spirit and truth must remain whether a song is to be sung to thousands or to a divine audience of One. I don't want to write songs that sound like songs we've already heard or songs that sound like the latest hit on the radio. I search for songs that bring a prophetically fresh sound, something straight from the Father's heart.

It is a magnificent night when we record a live album. That night is a snapshot of twelve months of growth in the heart of a local church that is fully determined to be all it is called to be. That recording catches a glimpse of a people hungry for more of God and desperate to bring His world into ours. I see this desire prevailing across the body of Christ more and more. This hunger for God is not exclusive to any particular church or denomination. His bride is eagerly waiting and preparing for the coming of her Beloved. We record because we want to lead all mankind into His glorious presence, encouraging them to sing songs from the depths of their hearts, expressing their thankfulness, joy, love, and devotion to God.

Keith Green was another magnificent writer of our time who wrote songs that helped spiritually shape an entire generation. "There Is a Redeemer" pierces me the core. I heard this prophetic word spoken over Russell Fragar: "And the angel of the Lord will stand at the foot of your bed at night and sing songs over you, O great scribe." What a divine way to write, to have songs sung to you straight from heaven that bring revelation, not just beautiful music. If we are trying to write the latest, greatest, biggest-selling album, then we have totally missed our purpose.

JESUS, WHAT A BEAUTIFUL NAME

JESUS, WHAT A BEAUTIFUL NAME
SON OF GOD, SON OF MAN
LAMB THAT WAS SLAIN
JOY AND PEACE, STRENGTH AND HOPE
GRACE THAT BLOWS ALL FEAR AWAY
JESUS, WHAT A BEAUTIFUL NAME

JESUS, WHAT A BEAUTIFUL NAME
TRUTH REVEALED, MY FUTURE SEALED
HEALED MY PAIN
LOVE AND FREEDOM, LIFE AND WARMTH
GRACE THAT BLOWS ALL FEAR AWAY
JESUS, WHAT A BEAUTIFUL NAME

JESUS, WHAT A BEAUTIFUL NAME
RESCUED MY SOUL, MY STRONGHOLD
LIFTS ME FROM SHAME
FORGIVENESS, SECURITY, POWER AND LOVE
GRACE THAT BLOWS ALL FEAR AWAY
JESUS, WHAT A BEAUTIFUL NAME

1995 TANYA RICHES/HILLSONG PUBLISHING

We are not an industry or a "marketplace." We are God's church, and we have the astounding responsibility of putting the sound of praise and worship into people's mouths.

George Frideric Handel's (1685–1759) "The Messiah" is one of the greatest musical accounts of the Gospel ever composed, and it still has a profound impact on the world to this day. Handel showed an unmistakable bent for music at a young age, but his father had other plans for George's life. He was determined that his son would be a lawyer and deemed music to be "an undignified sort of amusement." His father did everything he could to keep all musical instruments out of his son's reach and even kept George from going to school to avoid exposure to music lessons. But George Handel had an insatiable desire to play and managed to hide a rickety old spinet (a weak-sounding piano) in the attic. While the rest of the household slept, George played the instrument and exercised his tiny fingers over its keys until they ached. He succeeded in teaching himself to play before anyone knew anything about it. George was only seven years old.

One day he crept into the Duke of Saxe-Weissenfels Chapel to play the organ, not knowing anyone would be around. The Duke himself heard him play, and being a musical man, he immediately recognized the musical prodigy that was playing so magnificently before him. He took charge, ordering George's father to send him to music studies at once. What divine intervention—praise God for the Duke! "The Messiah" touched heaven and changed earth!

> *Sing to the Lord a new song, for he has done marvelous things . . .*
> *Shout for joy to the Lord, all the earth, burst into jubilant song with*
> *music; make music to the Lord with the harp, with the harp and the*
> *sound of singing, with trumpets and the blast of the ram's horn—shout*
> *for joy before the Lord, the King. (Psalm 98:1, 4–6)*

Psalm 40:3 says, "He put a new song in my mouth, a hymn of praise to our God. Many will see and fear and put their trust in the Lord."

We sing new songs at Hillsong Church week after week! The Word repeatedly exhorts us to bring a new song to the Lord. To sing a new song is to be fresh in your love for Him, fresh in your revelation of His Word.

If you write worship and praise songs, here are some practical keys I have learned that may help you:

1. Write songs that reflect what your pastor is teaching

Songs that reflect the current message to the church infiltrate listeners beyond their mind and affect their soul and spirit. Songs make the Word memorable and settle the message into our hearts. If you listen carefully to our Hillsong albums, you will hear a strong theme throughout the lyrics that most often were the result of Pastor Brian's messages.

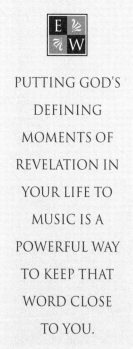

PUTTING GOD'S DEFINING MOMENTS OF REVELATION IN YOUR LIFE TO MUSIC IS A POWERFUL WAY TO KEEP THAT WORD CLOSE TO YOU.

Putting God's defining moments of revelation in your life to music is a powerful way to keep that Word close to you. An example of this is the song "What the Lord Has Done," which was written by Reuben Morgan to be sung at his own brother's water baptism. It reflects that beautiful moment in life when a man leaves his past behind and rises from the water into the new season God has reserved for him. The verse is beautiful:

And I will rise from waters deep
Into the saving arms of God
And I will sing salvation songs
Jesus Christ has set me free.

2. Make the songs easy for people to sing

When writing songs for the church, make sure people don't need to be Celine Dion or Michael Bolton in order to sing it. I hear many awe-inspiring songs, songs that are great for special presentations, but a song must be accessible to an untrained voice if we want the church to sing it.

3. Allow a memorable hook to develop

This is the repetitive, strong melody that drives home a point and allows the listener to easily participate. For example, in Miriam Webster's song "Dwelling Places," the lyrics "I love You, I love You, I love You" are powerful, and the melody is simple, which allows worshipers to easily understand the theme and take hold of it as their own.

4. Dig deeper when writing

Sometimes the first draft is the final form, but I encourage you to set it aside for a while. Then a day or more later, look at it again as though you had never seen it before. Dig for a new thought; explore a new expression lyrically to see if the wording can gain clarity and meaning. Take a prayerful, contemplative look at the song from start to finish.

5. Be agenda-free

Whatever we do for the Lord must come from the heart. Listen to Matt Redman's song "The Heart of Worship," and let the truth of his lyrics pierce your soul. It isn't possible to write for both the praises of man with its reward of money and at the same time bring the new sound and song that allows heaven to touch earth.

6. Be a big person

Allow room for constructive criticism. Some songs were only meant for you and the Lord. If you become too sensitive about your songs, you are in for a tough, long road ahead. Bounce your songs off someone you trust and then remember, the congregation is still the greatest road test for congregational songs. If after a few weeks the song doesn't fly— let it go! The greatest songs are *still* to be written, and the resource of our creative, expansive, generous, ever-loving God is inexhaustible!

Objectivity is an area where many songwriters get "knocked out" of the writing arena. Don't allow yourself to be wounded by criticism. Instead, accept it, learn from it, and move forward.

7. Always work on the skill of writing

Analyze music that you wouldn't normally listen to. Think outside of your own musical preferences. The greatest musicians and singers are the greatest listeners.

8. Go to the Word

Whenever I start writing, I open the Bible and sing and worship from a Psalm. There is nothing more inspiring.

> *Sing God a brand-new song!*
> *Earth and everyone in it, sing!*
> *Sing to God—worship God!*
> *Shout the news of his victory from sea to sea,*
> *Take the news of his glory to the lost,*
> *News of his wonders to one and all!*
> *For God is great, and worth a thousand Hallelujahs.*
> *—from Psalm 96* THE MESSAGE

Russell Fragar and I were once so determined to bring a new song of praise to church that even though we only had two hours, we wrote, charted, and had "That's What We Came Here For" ready just minutes before rehearsal started. The song took off, and that was that. We teach an average of thirty-five new songs annually, and the people in our church love it. But there have been moments when we have taught a song *quite badly!*

One night we were teaching a fresh new song to the church. In fact, it was a song that I had just written that afternoon. The band started the introduction, and it was beautiful. I took a breath, readied to start the verse, and couldn't remember exactly how it went. I signaled to the band to just keep playing the introduction, while I searched my memory bank for the starting line.

By the time we repeated the introduction another couple of times, it was becoming ridiculous, so I turned to the church and said, "I have absolutely no idea how this new song goes!" Everyone enjoyed a good laugh, while I searched the stage trying to find someone who remembered the song that I had just taught during rehearsal. Thank God, one of the musicians started to sing the first line into my ear. My brain reappeared, we started the song, the church cheered, we continued to worship, and we had an awesome night in the house of the Lord.

The strongest praise and worship songs are Scripture put to music, purely because the Bible is the living, breathing, infallible Word of God. Songs that are about our expression and feelings toward God are very intimate and, sadly, can receive a bit of criticism. But we have had thousands of pieces of communication from men and women of all ages saying thank-you for these personal songs: "I could never have expressed these thoughts I have toward the Lord like you have enabled me to." I honestly feel that these songs have had a strategic role in bringing a new sense of intimacy in people's relationship with the Lord. I love to sing about the majesty and the wonder of God, and it is wonderful to be able to express this through words of intimate devotion to Him.

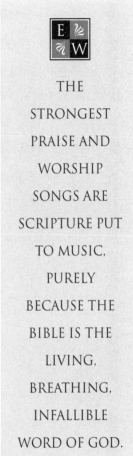

THE STRONGEST PRAISE AND WORSHIP SONGS ARE SCRIPTURE PUT TO MUSIC, PURELY BECAUSE THE BIBLE IS THE LIVING, BREATHING, INFALLIBLE WORD OF GOD.

WORTHY IS THE LAMB

THANK YOU FOR THE CROSS, LORD
THANK YOU FOR THE PRICE YOU PAID
BEARING ALL MY SIN AND SHAME
IN LOVE YOU CAME
AND GAVE AMAZING GRACE
THANK YOU FOR THIS LOVE, LORD
THANK YOU FOR THE NAIL-PIERCED HANDS
WASH ME IN YOUR CLEANSING FLOW
NOW ALL I KNOW
YOUR FORGIVENESS AND EMBRACE
WORTHY IS THE LAMB
SEATED ON THE THRONE
CROWN YOU NOW WITH MANY CROWNS
YOU REIGN VICTORIOUS
HIGH AND LIFTED UP
JESUS, SON OF GOD
THE DARLING OF HEAVEN CRUCIFIED
WORTHY IS THE LAMB
WORTHY IS THE LAMB

2001 DARLENE ZSCHECH/HILLSONG PUBLISHING

Chapter Ten

ETERNAL
HOME

ETERNAL HOME

The house of God is not about buildings and things; it's about the people, the body of all believers, who are the church. They are heaven's pride and joy, coming together to make His name famous and His praise glorious.

> *I am asking God for one thing, only one thing:*
> *To live with him in his house my whole life long.*
> *I'll contemplate His beauty; I'll study at His feet.*
> *That's the only quiet, secure place in a noisy world.*
> *(Psalm 27:4 THE MESSAGE)*

As an individual believer, I am His house. He lives in me, and in Him I have my purpose. But there is a dynamic life that is only found within the kingdom, when the "lovers of God" come together in unity to become the church—the glorious, unblemished, whole, beautiful bride for whom the King is returning. I believe that God is restoring praise and worship to His church, *and* at the same time He is restoring His church, His bride. He is restoring us to be what we were created to be—the hands and feet of Jesus. Collectively, we come together to create a structure that is made up of the powerful testimonies of His people.

We are entering a significant season in the kingdom of God. Can you sense it in the Holy Spirit? People are being saved in unprecedented numbers around the earth such as we have never seen before. God is causing His church to resist the crowd mentality of conforming to world standards and is anointing His bride to become radiant with His glory. We see signs and wonders following the preaching of the Word; the intimacy and powerful presence of God in corporate worship is becoming stronger and stronger.

There is a genuine abundance of joy both in the house of the Lord and in our individual daily lives. The light in the church is starting to draw attention to itself, and the world wants to know what is happening in the house of God.

IN GOD'S HOUSE THERE IS ROOM FOR EVERY ONE OF US TO FIND A PLACE TO SERVE, TO FLOURISH, AND TO GROW IN HIM.

I have a revelation of the church that I defend, love, and honor. The church isn't the building; the church is the people. The house is the covering of the church—it's the shelter, the refuge, the sanctuary. I have found in my travels that there are those who love the King and participate in the church under the banner of "worship and creative arts," but they don't love the house of the Lord. People who don't love their responsibility to the house of the Lord, the corporate gathering of the local church, will most likely disappoint the testimony of God's glory. Because hypocrisy is easy to find in the house of God, people become weary of investing their lives in service to their local church. But I have learned to trust in God and not man. I encourage you to do the same.

"Some trust in chariots and some in horses, but we trust in the name of the Lord our God" (Psalm 20:7). God will *NEVER* let you down. Don't fear the "what ifs" of serving in the church, the things you may have to die to. Start to dream about the "what could be's" if you actually sowed your life into something bigger than yourself! *You* can have a revelation of the power of the house of God. *You* can have a revelation of the church. Here are a few keys to being effective and fulfilled while serving in the great house of God.

REMEMBER, THERE IS ROOM FOR EVERYONE

John 10:10 says, "I have come that they may have *life*, and have it to the full" (emphasis added). Church is about the commitment and dedication you bring to the family of God. When the house of the Lord is operating as it should, it is flourishing, growing, successful, far-reaching, influential, embracing, and challenging! When the house of the Lord is not doing what it was born to do, it is containing, limiting, and frustrating. And if your local house is dysfunctional, there won't be anyone to cheer you on in your calling and offering of gifts to the Lord!

But in God's house there is room for every one of us to find a place to serve, to flourish, and to grow in Him. In the house of God we will live life in all its fullness. In fact, *The Message* describes it beautifully: "abundant, gracious and spacious . . . a spacious God-filled life." And there is room for your gift and for everyone else's in God's house. Psalm 52:8 says, "I am like an olive tree flourishing in the house of God." Personally, my life was always moving forward as a Christian, but it wasn't until I was deeply *planted* in the house of God that I began to flourish!

YOU CAN'T BUILD ON A FOUNDATION OF DOUBT, FEAR, OR UNBELIEF

You either trust God with your life or you don't! He puts people in authority over you, and it's your role to honor and serve without grumbling or feeling like you are missing out. No man (working in opposition) can interfere with God's divine appointment and His divine timing for you—only you can do that! When you are working through the principle of being "faithful in little" (Luke 16:10), you need to love the "little" part. Don't just bear the small beginnings as "marking time." Serving the

Lord's house is a heart decision. God loves His house and will do all to defend it.

Nehemiah 10:39 says, "We will not neglect the house of our God." We are to treasure it, prize it, and give our lives away for it. This is the secret to walking in His way and finding His purpose and plan that is beyond anything you could ever ask or think. Serving the house of the Lord is not a journey of fear; it is a journey using your faith to serve others.

DON'T FIGHT THE SILENT YEARS

Even Jesus was faithful to serve and to do his silent years of training well. The Word says, "Then he went down to Nazareth with them and was obedient to them. But his mother treasured all these things in her heart. And Jesus grew in wisdom and stature, and in favor with God and men" (Luke 2:51–52). Jesus didn't have a worldwide ministry. He fetched water and did whatever His parents asked Him to do. He was faithful in the everyday things.

Fighting for your time, your place, your voice, or your importance will always hinder your effectiveness in the great house of God. If you are faithful with what belongs to somebody else, God will give you your own. The testing ground is when you are being a loyal steward over what belongs to someone else. These are the silent years, the needful, precious, unseen years. The silent years bring a depth of devotion that cannot be found in "quick fixes." Silent years that are done well build a foundation of *trust* between yourself and the Lord that is not easily shaken.

Worship is precious to God's own heart, and it is no wonder that He works on our inner man continually as we worship Him, because He wants to trust us with so much. I am personally grateful for the unseen years when God's hand steadfastly corrected me, preparing me for the future. God is the ultimate Father. In the great house of God, remember, there is a time when all things will come together for His purpose, but there is also a way of obedience that brings it about!

Young men, in the same way, be submissive to those who are older. All of you, clothe yourselves with humility toward one another, because "God opposes the proud but gives grace to the humble." Humble yourselves, therefore, under God's mighty hand, that he may lift you up in due time. Cast all your anxiety on him because he cares for you.
(1 Peter 5:5–7)

GREATNESS BEGINS WITH WHOLEHEARTEDNESS

In 2 Chronicles, Solomon often refers to the wholehearted devotion of King David and the men and women of God who served in the house of the Lord. A wholehearted approach to service releases God's hand. The Scripture here talks about King Amaziah and his reign. The first half of the record of Amaziah's life is about his victory and his obedience to God, and the second half is about his defeat and his disobedience. In the middle of the book of 2 Chronicles, I noticed the transitional Scripture that speaks of Amaziah: "He did what was right in the eyes of the Lord, *but not wholeheartedly*" (2 Chronicles 25:2). I wondered whether or not his halfhearted attitude was the start of his decline. He was doing the right thing (he served well), but his approach was

A WHOLE-HEARTED APPROACH TO SERVICE RELEASES GOD'S HAND.

not wholehearted. King Amaziah's heart wandered, and he started to walk in disobedience.

MAGNIFICENT HOUSE OF GOD

THERE IS A HOUSE
DIFFERENT FROM ANY OTHER
FILLED WITH LIGHT AND LOVE
RADIANT WITH A GLORY THAT
IS TOTALLY IRRESISTIBLE TO ALL
IT'S AN OPEN HOME
A HUGE WELCOME SIGN HANGS FROM THE DOOR
INSIDE OVERFLOWS WITH GOOD FOOD
AND BOUNTIFUL SUPPLY
LAUGHTER AND HEALTHY CONVERSATION
AND FOR ALL WHO ARE QUESTIONING
THERE ARE ANSWERS
AN ABUNDANCE OF HOPE
SALVATION IS OFFERED TO ALL
MERCY AND GRACE KISS EACH ONE
A FIRE IS CRACKLING WITHIN ITS SOLID WALLS
ALWAYS THERE TO WARM AND SOOTHE
GENTLY DRYING TEARSTAINED FACES

AFFIRMING THE WANDERING SOUL…

AND BRINGING STRONG COUNSEL…

TO GIVE CLEAR DIRECTION TO ALL

NEGOTIATING THIS JOURNEY OF LIFE

CAPTIVATING MELODIES

FILL EVERY INCH OF EVERY ROOM

A NEW SOUND AVAILABLE

TO EVEN THE UNTRAINED EAR

CAUSING EVERY HEART TO WILLINGLY SING

AND EVERY KNEE TO HUMBLY BOW

THIS IS THE HOUSE I GIVE MY LIFE TO BUILD

TO GATHER HIS CHURCH…

AND TO BRING HEALING TO THE NATIONS

THIS IS THE ONLY HOUSE FIT FOR A KING

THIS IS THE MAGNIFICENT HOUSE OF GOD

God's hand is limited when your heart is misdirected. Anything you hope to do well needs to be approached wholeheartedly. If you want to live as an excellent worshiper in His house, you must approach Him with your whole heart—there is no other way.

ASK GOD TO TEACH YOU TO LOVE HIS HOUSE

Nothing is too hard when you are in love. Ask God to increase your ability to love what He loves and to love establishing His kingdom through building His great house. Acts 20:28 says, "Be shepherds of the church of God, which he bought with his own blood." He bought the church with His own blood—God's house matters.

Mark and I often think about why we love God's house so much and why we have given our lives to it. One night we wrote down the following reasons we are passionate for the church:

We Love God's Presence

God's house is the place where He lingers and loves to be adored.

We Love the Sense of Family

God's house gives us a sense of belonging. The church is not a club that excludes anyone because he or she did not come from the right background. It is a "come as you are, we love you, how are you doing?" kind of place. That rich sense of family is scarce elsewhere on earth.

It Is the Greatest Learning Ground for Life

Being planted in God's house developed the leadership skills that Mark and I have learned. Here we are prospering and learning to live a fulfilled, abundant life.

We Love Being Able to Give

We love to give into something that builds and restores lives, including our own. I love giving finances into the house of God, because I know I am sowing into great soil.

It's a Place Where Children Flourish

Week by week I am watching my children develop into individuals who are fully in love with Jesus. It is tremendous to watch your children thrive in the environment of a healthy house.

We Love Sharing Our Lives

The house of God is a place where Mark and I can share our lives, our dreams, and our future. We are convinced that God has blessed our marriage relationship because we have made a decision to build the house of God together.

We Love Seeing Our Gifts Released and Polished

The house of God is a healthy ground to release our talents and gifts, where they will be challenged and honed. Our gifts have been tested and our character continues to build as we sow who we are and what we do into the house.

We Love Our Friends in God's House

Friendships have been born and developed in the house of God that continually overwhelm us. We have the privilege of committed relationships that over time have stood the test, and we know they are friendships that will always be there.

Think about the house of God in which you are planted and consider what you can offer to the Lord's banquet table. Your gifts and talents will help make that house a place that honors the Lord on this earth today.

You can do it by knowing God and by pursuing unity with the body of believers who share the house of God. You can serve God and His house by loving discipline and excellence and by obediently bringing your gift to the table because of who God is.

THINK ABOUT THE HOUSE OF GOD IN WHICH YOU ARE PLANTED AND CONSIDER WHAT YOU CAN OFFER TO THE LORD'S BANQUET TABLE.

God's house is radiant, and His glory will be seen throughout the earth as thousands upon thousands of extravagant worshipers, worshiping in spirit and in truth and lifting a mighty roar of praise, continue to run to the ever-open arms of Jesus. I earnestly pray that you will live your life extravagantly for the cause of Christ. Let your thirst for His love and His purposes be unquenchable. Live extravagantly for Him so that the lost may know Him and so that the world will be drawn to the irresistible presence of the King. I believe the Father longs for His people to be extravagant worshipers. God has put us together on earth for this time and trusted us for this season of praise, so let's do it well.

Salvation Prayer

My prayer for you, dear friend, above all else, is that you come into divine relationship with the Author of love himself, Jesus Christ. Allow His perfect love to invade your life and take your breath away.

I surrendered my life to God's unconditional love at a young age and discovered that only His love had the capacity to present this once-broken young woman as whole. I now live with God as my Father, Jesus as my Savior, and the Holy Spirit as my best friend. I understand that this reality is overwhelming, but it is the truth.

"You shall know the truth, and the truth shall set you free" (John 8:32).

Welcoming Jesus into your life is as simple as praying a prayer. If you are not sure about your eternal destiny, then pray this prayer *today*:

> *Dear Lord Jesus,*
> *Today I confess my need of you.*
> *Thank you for dying on the cross*
> *so that I might have life.*
> *Thank you for forgiving me of my sins.*
> *Thank you for loving me,*
> *and thank you for the privilege of loving you.*
> *Please give me the strength to follow after you*
> *with all my heart and soul*
> *and to bring glory to your name.*
> *I commit my life into your hands.*
> *I will love you forever.*
> *Amen.*

If you have prayed this prayer for the first time or have surrendered your life to Christ anew, I would love to hear from you.

Please write to me at Hillsong Church, P.O. Box 1195, Castle Hill NSW 1765, Australia. E-mail address: *www.hillsong@hillsong.com*

Live to delight the heart of God.

I love you,

THE ZSCHECH FAMILY

**AMY, DARLENE, MARK, CHLOE
... AND BABY ZOE JEWEL**

AFTERWORD

My beautiful daughter Amy wore a size ten shoe by the time she was twelve! She is still growing, so we don't know what size she will wear when she reaches her full height. My feet are size eight and a half, and my mother's are a petite size six. Every generation is getting bigger and bigger than the previous one. They're also becoming stronger in many ways; they are more confident, zealous, fearless, and full of vision, with a *can do* attitude. If their incredibly focused behaviors are nurtured within a godly environment, the future of these courageous young people is magnificent!

*Let this be written for a future generation, that a people not yet
created may praise the Lord. (Psalm 102:18)*

Christian leaders have a responsibility to pass on all we know to the next generation of believers. We who have walked with God can boast of Him; we can commend His works to those running behind us; we can teach them how to value the journey and not to resent it; and we can show them that the only way to live life "to the max" is through knowing Christ. We are to tell this new generation of the awesome things God has done and to teach them about His faithfulness.

I have a personal conviction to lift up this generation of worshipers in the things of God. I want to provide a rich spiritual platform from which new worshipers can be launched. I want to see young worshipers doing exploits we never dared to dream about! I want to see extravagant worshipers be living examples and show the next generation how to give away their lives. I want to see excellent worshipers inspiring the next generation to live wholeheartedly for the Lord. There are millions of young people begging for leadership that is radical in its commitment and true to its word.

Does your life create a living, breathing journal of what is possible for those around you? If your personal confession is full of negative words—a "this is so hard" kind of vibe—or if your life is full of faithless stress, then your example will probably only repel those whom you have the opportunity to impact. Radical discipleship is needed! The key word here, much more than a mental list of rules and regulations, is *vision*.

Vision inspires.
Vision allows you to *see* the unseen.
Vision gets you doing things you *never dreamed*
of accomplishing.
Vision creates an environment in which a team
operates at its very best.
Vision pushes you to look past the obvious
and look to the supernatural.

To watch a vision come to pass only requires good eyesight. To actually birth a vision and then watch over its development to completion requires great faith, great strength, and great wisdom! It is one thing to have a vision, but it is another thing to communicate that vision and make it real for others so that they may run with it and make it their aspiration too.

One generation will commend your works to another; they will tell of your mighty acts. (Psalm 145:4)

King David was *impassioned* with a God-given vision to build the Jerusalem temple. He was determined to see it come to pass. He dreamed about it, talked about it, and spent months poring over designs and resource materials. The dream was his. Then the day came when God himself told David to pass on the task of building the temple to his son Solomon. David had to hand over the vision well, with enthusiasm, without regret, not holding anything back. David gave his son Solomon all the plans God had revealed to him (1 Chronicles 22:1–21).

David had reached a level of maturity in God. He had learned to obey with wholehearted energy. The lesson for us is great, for David imparted his passion, faith, and courage to Solomon, who represents the next generation to praise the Lord. His words to his son reflect the commission we now have to pass to new worshipers:

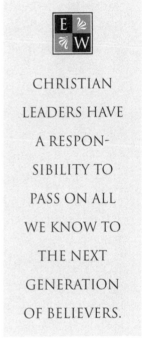

> David also said to Solomon his son, "Be strong and courageous, and do the work. Do not be afraid or discouraged, for the Lord God, my God, is with you. He will not fail you or forsake you until all the work for the service of the temple of the Lord is finished. The divisions of the priests and Levites are ready for all the work on the temple of God, and every willing man skilled in any craft will help you in all the work. The officials and all the people will obey your every command"
> (1 Chronicles 28:20–21).

CHRISTIAN LEADERS HAVE A RESPONSIBILITY TO PASS ON ALL WE KNOW TO THE NEXT GENERATION OF BELIEVERS.

David's selfless support and generous encouragement showed great strength of character. First Chronicles 29:3 says, "Besides, in my devotion to the temple of my God I now give my personal treasures of gold and silver for the temple of my God, over and above everything I have provided for this holy temple."

David's inspirational leadership continued as he gave of his personal treasure and wealth. His example of giving motivated the leaders of Israel to invest their personal treasure toward the building of the temple. King

David ultimately recognized that all things come from and belong to the Lord.

When imparting vision to those looking to you for direction, pour yourself into them, letting them know and see the things in life that are truly *valuable*.

Sometimes I watch these amazing young people on our worship team, who are *alive* with vision, who give everything, and who are God chasers; and I praise God for the opportunity of being able to contribute in some way to their development in becoming *extravagant worshipers*.

It's not always easy to mentor and equip the next generation, but that is precisely what we have been called to do. We have to be willing to do whatever it takes to see them increase and develop. We need to be willing to put the "ball" back in their hand when they drop it, and be ready for them to do things differently than we do. Don't give up if it takes them a little while to find their feet either. Learn to cover them when immaturity shows, when they make decisions or proceed with actions that are lacking in wisdom. Remember your own colorful journey to leadership.

When my friend was young and had been a Christian for just a few weeks, she asked her youth leader if she and a group of her newly saved friends could do a dance routine in the church. The youth leader was keen to encourage these beautiful new converts, and so without ever seeing or listening to what they were about to do, said, "Cool! Come dance for us all."

Well, the blood ran from his face as these innocent but extremely enthusiastic girls started dancing to *It's Raining Men* by The Weather Girls. The chorus says, "It's raining men, Hallelujah!" so the girls thought it was a godly song! Oops! The church was mortified, and yet somehow I can see all of heaven smiling and cheering as these new babes in Christ brought their offering!

I love to glean golden lessons for life from the lives of strong, godly men and women who have dedicated their lives to Him. Billy Graham's commitment to the call of God on his life has blown me away many times, reminding me to live my life totally on fire for God. In his book *Just As I Am,* there is a beautiful section where he reflects on his life in the ministry and gives great advice to those running their race behind him. He says, "I would also spend more time in spiritual nurture, seeking to grow closer to God so I could become more like Christ. I would spend more time in prayer, not just for myself, but for others" (N.Y.: Harper-Collins, 1997).

In his book he talks about being in great demand as a preacher and how he learned to negotiate success in ministry. Billy Graham also mentions that he would have spent more time with his family: "Every day I was absent from my family is gone forever. Although much of that travel was necessary, some of it was not." What a valuable lesson to learn. His consecrated life has challenged me on many levels and thoroughly inspires me.

I *adore* my family. To be a mother is one of life's absolute greatest gifts. As I sit and write this, I am holding my brand-new baby daughter, Zoe Jewel. Words can't describe what I feel for her; she is just too lovely, so totally luscious. Many people ask me, "How do you do it? How do you combine marriage, motherhood, and ministry?"

For years I tried to juggle all the elements of life. I knew there was a God call on my life to be in ministry, and yet I also knew that it could never be at the expense of my family. When I tried to juggle *all* the boxes, I learned the hard way that it is difficult to keep them from all crashing down. So I no longer have boxes for marriage, ministry, and motherhood. Instead, God has shown me that there is a divine order for my life. Instead of trying to make sure that everything is balanced (there is no prescribed formula of balance), God showed me that I am to break out of the box mentality and instead seek Him for *divine order* for my day. Each day differs from the day before. The dynamics change, but the call on my life doesn't. Marriage, motherhood, and ministry are all cohesively part of that call. God anoints us for our entire call. (I must write another book on this.)

God's Word says, "Train up a child in the way he should go, and when he is old, he will not depart from it" (Proverbs 22:6). Mark and I put our trust in this passage of Scripture as our parental blueprint to raise our gorgeous girls as people who love and value the house of God and all that the King's house represents. But recently I saw this Scripture in a new light. My heart is to train and teach the Christian musicians and singers to dedicate themselves wholly to the mission of the kingdom. I want to lead them to their own personal revelation of the honor and privilege of serving in the King's house, which is the greatest honor of all for any singer or musician. I want to train up worshipers to serve the Lord with gladness and to break the mold on what is traditionally accepted behavior of a "creative" person.

Every brand-new baby born into this world is born looking for food, searching for the best nourishment that they innately know will sustain them. Once children taste the best food, they are ruined for anything less! As I viewed the wonder of my newborn baby eager to be fed and my sense of fulfillment from feeding her only food that is full of nutrients needed to keep her delicate new being healthy and satisfied, I understood more clearly my mission to help babes in Christ taste the goodness of God and to see them saturated in His manifest presence. I want to mentor the next generation of worshipers and replace the mystery that has clouded their thoughts over the years with God encounters. Once believers have tasted and seen that the Lord is good, once they have sensed the smile of God as their worship offering melts His heart, once they learn that His Word *cannot* lie and will prevail over *all* else, they are ruined for anything less than His presence.

Once a believer has tasted the goodness of God's presence in worship, playing music for music's sake brings a frustration that is hard to explain to anyone who hasn't tasted of heaven. When worshipers won't settle for anything less than the best of God's presence, we have achieved our goal of mentoring the next generation of extravagant worshipers. As we mentor the next generation, we are entrusted to point them to the reality of Jesus. They may try for a season to "color outside the lines," but eventually their taste buds will only be truly satisfied by the divine honor of serving Christ.

Even when I am old and gray, do not forsake me, O God, till I declare
your power to the next generation, your might to all who are to come.
(Psalm 71:18)

One time when I was away on a ministry trip, we had just finished a whole night of praise and worship, and then we gave an altar call. It was fantastic to see many people walk forward to accept Christ. When a man in his late seventies walked forward and started to sob, God gave me a picture of the generations behind him that his decision would affect. It makes me cry just to think about how he sobbed before the Lord. He took a step of obedience that wasn't just for him, that wasn't just for his seed, but that would change the seed of the generations to come. I was so excited for him. He couldn't see it because he was just being born of the Spirit at that moment. But as he stood there, I watched him change the generations.

As we become extravagant worshipers today, we will change the next generation of believers—the Jesus Generation, radical in their service, radical in their commitment, and tomorrow's extravagant worshipers.

BELIEVE

I SAY ON SUNDAY HOW MUCH I WANT REVIVAL
BUT THEN BY MONDAY, I CAN'T EVEN FIND MY BIBLE
WHERE'S THE POWER
THE POWER OF THE CROSS IN MY LIFE
I'M SICK OF PLAYING THE GAME OF RELIGION
I'M TIRED OF LOSING MY REASON FOR LIVING
WHERE'S THE POWER
THE POWER OF THE CROSS IN MY LIFE
I'M NOT CONTENT JUST TO WALK THROUGH MY LIFE
GIVING IN TO THE LIES
WALKING IN COMPROMISES
NOW WE CRY OUT AS A GENERATION THAT WAS LOST
BUT NOW IS FOUND IN THE POWER OF THE CROSS
WE BELIEVE IN YOU, WE BELIEVE IN THE POWER
OF YOUR WORD AND ITS TRUTH
WE BELIEVE IN YOU SO WE LAY DOWN OUR CAUSE
THAT OUR CROSS MIGHT BE FOUND IN YOU
I'M NOT SATISFIED DOING IT MY OWN WAY
I'M NOT SATISFIED TO DO CHURCH AND WALK AWAY
I'M NOT SATISFIED, THERE'S NO LOVE IN MY LIFE BUT YOU
I'M NOT SATISFIED LIVING IN YESTERDAY'S HOUR
I'M NOT SATISFIED TO HAVE THE FORM,
BUT NOT THE POWER
I'M NOT SATISFIED, OH, LORD, I AM CRUCIFIED IN YOU

1999 DONNA LASIT/CITY BIBLE PUBLISHING**

Mercy
Ministries
AUSTRALIA

A few years ago, during a trip to the USA, Mark and I were introduced to
Nancy Alcorn, the founder of Mercy Ministries. On that day, God breathed
life into a long-time dream that we'd held carefully in our hearts...
to be involved in seeing broken lives restored, and lovingly put back together by
the immeasurable power of our awesome Lord.

I encourage you to join with us in supporting this valuable work.

Mark & Darlene Zschech

Mercy Ministries provides support for young women struggling with
eating disorders, drug & alcohol abuse and unplanned pregnancy.
Care is given absolutely free of charge, and includes practical training
in areas such as budgeting, nutrition and fitness, as well as specific
counselling for each girl's needs. Together, we see these beautiful
young women emerge confident, and full of hope for the future.

MERCY MINISTRIES AUSTRALIA. PH: 1800 011 537, PO BOX 1537
CASTLE HILL, NSW 1765, AUSTRALIA, WWW.MERCYMINISTRIES.COM.AU

MERCY MINISTRIES OF AMERICA, PH: (615) 831 6987, PO BOX 111060
NASHVILLE, TN 37222-1060 USA, WWW.MERCYMINISTRIES.COM

Everyone wants the best for their children... that's why I sponsor two girls with Compassion. Our two sponsored girls receive health care, food, education and importantly... hear the Gospel through their local church. It's a joy to receive their letters and be involved in their lives.

By sponsoring a child through Compassion you really will make a difference — to the child and to the community. Just think of the difference we can make if we all sponsor a child.

Darlene Zschech

TO FIND OUT MORE ABOUT HOW YOU CAN
SPONSOR A CHILD, PLEASE CONTACT
COMPASSION TODAY.

PH: 1800 224 453 WWW.COMPASSIONAUST.COM.AU
WWW.COMPASSION.COM.